THE
INTELLECT
—and—
BEYOND

THE
INTELLECT
—and—
BEYOND

OLIVER R. BARCLAY

Academie Books Grand Rapids, Michigan
Zondervan Publishing House

101299

THE INTELLECT AND BEYOND
Copyright © 1985 by The Zondervan Corporation
Grand Rapids, Michigan

This is a revised edition of *Developing a Christian Mind*, published by Inter-Varsity Press, Leicester, UK.

Library of Congress Cataloging in Publication Data

Barclay, Oliver R.
    The intellect and beyond

    Revision of: Developing a Christian mind.
    1. Intellect—Religious aspects—Christianity.
2 Christian life—1960–   I. Barclay, Oliver R.
Developing a Christian mind.   II. Title.
BV4509.5.B37   1985   248   85–23621.

ISBN 0-310-33291-5

Edited by LaVonne Neff
Designed by Louise Bauer

Printed in the United States of America

85 86 87 88 89 / 10 9 8 7 6 5 4 3 2 1

Contents

Introduction

Having a Christian mind is important in the New Testament. Of that there is no doubt. Jesus himself told us to give attention to it. But what exactly is a Christain mind, and how does it work in practice? Does it mean that we have to become intellectuals? Certainly not. It will have an intellectual aspect for intellectual people, of course, but I want to show that in the New Testament it is something very practical and down to earth.

Because our minds are involved in the simplest decisions, the challenge to develop a Christian mind is something we cannot escape. Every Christian who has been spiritually renewed has, as I hope to show, a new mind to a considerable extent. Our task is to love God with *all* our minds. We are either obedient or disobedient in the matter. Either we try to please God by loving him with all out minds or we shirk this responsibility, hoping that somehow a mindless love will be good enough.

We must not be misled on the one hand by those who despise a Christian mind and regard it as merely an optional extra for those so inclined or on the other hand by those who make it a highly rarefied affair for academics only. In the Bible it is for everybody: fishermen, soldiers, farmers, tax collectors, philosophers, and religious leaders alike. It applies as much to the uneducated slave as to his educated master, to the Greek philosopher as to the Jewish peasant.

The plan of the book is as follows. In the first five chapters I try to make sure that in talking about the "Christian mind" or the "renewed mind" we are talking about the same ideal as is intended in the Bible and that we give it the same kind of practical relevance that the Bible gives to it. The Bible uses the concept in ways that surprise some people. In the next three chapters I develop three areas of application in a fuller way. They are only samples, but they aim to show the kind of way in which the renewed mind enables us to capture more ground for Christ in our lives and in our society.

In writing a book such as this, one is bound to be indebted to many people, sometimes without being altogether aware of the debt. I hope that my friends will recognize themes and ideas that they have either sharpened up for me or planted in my mind in the first place, and will take the credit for what is good in the result. My thanks, however, are due most particularly to my wife for her constant help, criticism, and encouragement, including the transcribing of some most difficult manuscript and typing most of the book at some stage. Mrs. Pamela Mason did most of the rest of the typing, and others have helped in other ways. I offer my sincere thanks to them all.

1

What is a Christian mind?

The Christian mind is not necessarily an intellectual affair. Indeed, we are warned in the Bible and church history that the attempt to be intellectual can lead away from, and not nearer to, a Christian mind. Thinking by Christians that has not been really "converted" has enormous possibilities for evil. This book is not primarily a plea for Christians to think—we all have to do that if we are human beings! It is a plea that, when we think, we think Christianly. Great damage is done when devout Christians fail in this, even if the failure is excused by a plea that to think too much is unspiritual. This is simply to leave the field to unspiritual thinking on the one hand and to our own fallen human impulses and feelings on the other. The Bible insists that our hearts and minds must be changed. Indeed the word *repentance* means a change of *mind*, not merely a change of behavior. The right path, then, is not merely intellectual effort—it is *Christian* thinking. This is every bit as important in the Christian life as Christian feeling or emotion.

Love God with all your mind

What, then, is a Christian mind? The idea goes back to Jesus himself, and we had better start there. The introduction of the word "mind" is itself surprising. When he was asked which was the greatest commandment, he replied that it was "You shall love the Lord your God with all your heart, and with all your soul, and with all your mind, and with all your strength" (Mark 12:30). Here he quotes Deuteronomy 6:4. The Old Testament passage itself, however, does not include the word "mind." It says, "with all your heart, and with all your soul, and with all your might [or strength]." Both in this passage and in Luke, a fourth term "mind" is deliberately added (in Matt. 22:37 "mind" is again added to "heart" and "soul").

This is very significant. The explanation is that the range of meaning of the Hebrew word translated "heart" had narrowed so much that in Greek two words, "heart and mind," were needed to say what was covered in the Old Testament by the one word "heart." But whereas the official Greek translation of the Old Testament, the Septuagint, gives a strictly literal translation and uses only the three words, the New Testament takes great care to show the range of the term and therefore includes the word for "mind" as a *necessary* part of our love for God. This shows how important it is that out minds be made to play their part in true devotion and loving service to God. The Christian who will not seek to love God with all his mind—as well as with his heart and soul and strength—is a sadly defective Christian. All our faculties are affected by sin and all are equally to be renewed and brought into the service of God.

Having a Christian mind is therefore no small thing. It is part of the first and greatest commandment, and, as we hope to show, it comes in a place in the whole scheme of Christian salvation which makes it crucial to both Christian conduct and Christian character as well as to Christian thought. If we do not worship and serve God with a truly renewed mind we shall fail sadly in worship as well as in daily life and other aspects of service. This is also something we are *commanded* to do. It is not just an optional extra for the more intellectual. The early church members who were told to have a renewed mind were mostly uneducated and simple people, many of them slaves and probably illiterate. They needed a Christian mind as much as anyone. And we must not avoid the challenge today if we are to be New Testament Christians. This needs emphasis at the present time, because the current culture of the Western world is tending to put feelings so much before thinking that it has in some circles become hard to defend Christian thinking at all. But Christ wants the whole of us to be in his service. It is of virtually no value to be transformed merely in our thinking if the gospel has not touched our hearts. But a Christian experience that is only in the heart and has not renewed our mind is both inadequate and also, according to Jesus, deeply at fault. It lacks repentance, and its love is incomplete.

A renewed mind in practice

To take just one further biblical example, in Romans 12:1–2, after a careful setting out of eleven chapters of Christian doctrine and the whole scheme of salvation and growth in Christian character, Paul makes this appeal: "I appeal to you therefore, brethren, by the mercies of God [i.e., by the truth of the gospel set out in chapters 1–11], to present your bodies as a living sacrifice, holy and acceptable to God, which is your spiritual worship. Do not be conformed to this world but be *transformed* by the *renewal of your mind*, that you may prove what is the will of God, what is good and acceptable and perfect." It is a powerful *command* that has been translated as "Don't let the world around you squeeze you into its mold, but let God remold your minds" (J. B. Phillips' translation). Paul is showing that, unless the mind is really renewed, we shall not be transformed in life and character as we should be and are likely to retain much of an un-Christian, worldly outlook. We could be transformed in heart and soul (which earlier chapters of Romans deal with), but still come tragically short of what God wants for us and commands us to be. At this stage, therefore, he adds that we must be transformed in mind before he goes on in chapters 12–16 to the transformation of our life and character, because that can come about only in that way.

The instrument of our transformation is the renewed mind. Romans 12, in fact, following the verses we have discussed, goes on immediately in verse 3, not to some abstract area of thought, but to a far more shattering application of the renewed mind. If you are not familiar with the passage, I invite you to stop for a moment and ask what you think the first kind of application might be. To worship? To daily life? To social or political or church life? To a critique of modern pagan thought? Let Paul speak. "By the grace given to me I beg every one among you not to think of himself more highly than he ought to think." The first result of a Christian mind in this passage is to have a proper attitude about yourself. The gospel cuts you down to size. It does not lead to regarding yourself as insignificant before God, "but to think with sober judgment, each according to the measure of faith which God has assigned him." It does, however, totally undermine self-centeredness and makes you concerned instead for God's glory. It is a marvelous medicine in an age when to do your own thing, or to seek job satisfaction or satisfaction in your relationships, is the first priority of most people.

Paul's next theme is to urge the readers to seek to serve others in love according to whatever gifts God has given them (v. 6). That is a fundamental part of the Christian mind. Without it we have missed the priorities in Christian thinking. To take another biblical example, Paul writes in Philippians 2:3–7,

> "Do nothing from selfishness or conceit, but in humility count others better than yourselves. Let each of you look not only to his own interests, but also to the interests of others. Have this *mind* among yourselves, which is yours in Christ Jesus, who, though he was in the form of God, did not count equality with God a thing to be grasped, but emptied himself, taking the form of a servant, being born in the likeness of men."

A Christian mind is here again seen to start with humility and a desire to serve rather than to be important or comfortable. According to the New Testament this is the first application of the Christian mind. Unless a Christian mind leads to humility, to a proper deflation of our self-estimate and a proper dethronement of our selfish concerns for our own interests, a well-developed piece of Christian thinking in some academic field will be a hollow achievement.[1]

When the missionaries Dr. and Mrs. John Coleman were held as prisoners by the authorities in Iran for a year, people all over the world were praying for their release. This is perfectly proper and has New Testament precedent, but Dr. Coleman tells that this was not his own concern. He did not pray for his own release. In the first place, he did not wish to be released unless the Iranian pastors of his church, who were also in prison, were released at the same time. Secondly, he had gone to Iran to serve the people, and if he could do so to some extent in prison, that was an opportunity not to be despised. If he was deported he would lose the opportunity. His concern was not to be comfortable or safe, but to live for God's glory and to ensure that he gave a Christian witness in all circumstances. He was more concerned that he react to these circumstances in a truly Christian way than that he be delivered from them. It is true that he was accused falsely and detained without trial. He could have entered into a deep discussion about the role of the state. Indeed, he may have done so. But his having a Christian mind was demonstrated as much by his view of himself and his own captivity and possible release as it would have been by his defending his rights to freedom or in a well-worked-out Christian view of the state.

The recent debate

This discussion is not at all new. It has had to be tackled afresh in each culture and in each generation. In the 1960s Harry Blamires started another round of the debate by publishing his

[1]Where the English versions use the one word for "mind" the Greek uses several. In Romans 12 and Ephesians 4 it is chiefly *nous*, which is perhaps a rather more intellectual concept. In Philippians 2 and Romans 8 it is *phronēma*, which is more attitudinal. In Matthew, Mark, and Luke it is *dianoia*, which some describe as the products of thinking rather than thinking itself. In 2 Corinthians 10 and 11 it is *noēma*. But the differences are small if they are even meant to be significant, and Romans 12 seems to move deliberately from *nous* to *phroneō*. The English word "outlook" covers them all; see pp. 15, 57)

book *The Christian Mind*, with its scathing attacks on the platitudes and compromises that often do duty for "Christian statement." That book is still influential. His plea for more rigorous and truly Christian statements met with widespread agreement, but no one seemed to be able to show how to go ahead from there and to apply his thinking to any wide range of concerns. After a lot of discussion that did not seem to lead anywhere, many became disillusioned. They began to ask whether the ideal of a Christian mind was not a will-o'-the-wisp. I believe that one reason for this is that Blamires's definition of a Christian mind is essentially more theoretical than the New Testament concept. He defines it as follows: "a set of notions and attitudes." There are some excellent passages in the book which might imply a less exclusively intellectual concept, but his definition won the day.

Whether he intended it or not, the result was that many people took it as a challenge to develop a complete intellectual system of a kind that existed in the medieval times that Blamires so much admired. That sort of system, as I hope to show, is not what the New Testament asks of us. The Bible is thinking of something else and gives us a clear idea of what it is and how we are to move toward it. I believe that the "set of notions" ideal is in truth a will-o'-the-wisp and that, if we insist on looking for it as the main feature of a Christian mind, we shall end in disillusionment again. Those Christian thinkers who have simply adopted Blamires's definition, or something similar (and there are quite a few), are likely also to lead us into disillusionment because they raise expectations that they cannot fulfill. More important than that, however, is the question whether such a view of the Christian mind captures the biblical emphasis at all.

Blamires and some other writers enjoy arguing that there simply is no Christian mind today, and, on his definition, one can see why he thinks that is true. I want to argue, however, that, in the New Testament sense, every Christian has a Christian mind to some extent, or he cannot be a Christian at all. Anyone born of the Spirit of God and reading the Bible has his outlook on himself and his life deeply changed. As Paul puts it in Romans 8:5–10, "Those who live according to the Spirit set their *minds* on the things of the Spirit." Our failure in this area is that we do not allow our mind to be *more deeply* Christian—as much about our attitude to marriage and our job as to the most learned problems raised by a confrontation with non-Christian thoughts; as much about our mother-in-law and our money as about our pride and our philosophy. There may not be a Christian consensus in politics or social affairs or education or apologetics. But those concerns are only a small part of what is covered by a Christian mind. We have all made a start. The New Testament challenges us to be *thoroughly* renewed in mind as an essential part of growing up as Christians to serve and please God.

Toward a definition of a Christian mind

Let me then attempt a preliminary definition of the Christian mind as I believe the idea is presented in the New Testament, so that we may clearly understand what we are talking about. I shall then go on in the rest of the book to examine it further and to look at some of the ways in which it works out. I shall be asking what happens when we try to obey God by loving him with all our mind.

Although the actual phrase "a Christian mind" is not used in the Bible, the New Testament does claim for the Christian that he has "the mind of Christ," and in the passages we have looked at we are urged, even commanded, to be "renewed in our minds" and to "have this mind among yourselves, which is yours in Christ Jesus." If this is thought of in an exclusively intellectual way, we shall be at fault in one direction, and if we use it in an exclusively personal way—out attitude to ourselves before God, which indeed comes first—we shall sadly miss the thrust of the New Testament in the other direction. My preliminary definition, then, is as follows. By a Christian mind I believe the Bible means "a Christian outlook that controls our life and our thinking." I shall try to show that the word "outlook" comes nearer to the New Testament concept than the word "mind" in its present usage, and that it is a practical and devotional idea as well as an intellectual one. I shall, however, hope to put more body into this concept as we go along. Let me at this juncture say only that I do not believe that we should allow the phrase "Christian thinking," any more than the expression "a Christian mind," to be given a highly intellectual or academic meaning. It can include that, and it does for those so gifted. But even an uneducated child has to think, for thinking is a fundamental human function, and it is in terms of striving for a Christian outlook that our Lord and the New Testament writers talk about the mind to illiterate slaves as well as to others. Perhaps "Christian thinking" would do as a definition if it were not inevitable that many people today would give it too intellectual a content. That is why I have preferred the word "outlook" and have stressed its application in my definition. But I shall return to this later.

My point is well illustrated by the fact that in one place Paul deliberately expresses the idea of a renewed Christian mind by saying, "Be renewed in the *spirit* of your minds" (Eph. 4:23). What he is talking about evidently means a radical change of outlook and of inward attitudes and priorities in life, as well as a framework of thoughts or, to use Blamires's word, "notions." We are being called to change our whole outlook on ourselves, our life, our friends, our society, and then the whole world. We are to see things with new eyes and then to work out the implications.

Its present-day urgency

The whole subject did not seem so urgent when the majority of people accepted (at least in theory) Christian priorities and Christian morals. It was not so long ago that people used to say, "We all believe in the Sermon on the Mount." Few people would dream of saying that today. Nowadays we are constantly reminded of the fact that there is a sharp contrast between Christian and non-Christian values. The world around us, even in Western "Christendom," is controlled by Christian tradition. Thinking that is really hostile to a Christian outlook is often taken for granted in the media, in the whole educational process, and in the ordinary relationships of life. It easily invades the church. Christian views of marriage, family life, money, Sunday, and even truth and honesty are regarded as totally out of date. It is not so much that these things are actually attacked. It is rather that un-Christian attitudes on these and many other matters are taken for granted, and, by a sort of osmosis, our thinking, and as a result our lives, are in danger of becoming less and less Christian if we do not take active steps to counter them. Marital unfaithfulness, for instance, is taken for granted. Dishonesty with income tax returns and subtle materialism are part of the normal way of thinking in our society. Businessmen speak as if they were in business simply to make money irrespective of worldly or social harm. "That," we are told "is the name of the game" (see chapter 7).

This, of course, was exactly the situation of the early church to which the New Testament Epistles were written. It is obvious that not only were these early Christians surrounded by decisively non-Christian ways of thinking and living, but that many of the church members had been part of that society and had shared its outlook. They now had to make a decisive break with their past and had to start developing a completely new life. That necessitated a change of mind. Today, as then, we need to have a Christian mind and also be able to say what that means by contrast with the accepted outlook of our society. We need to be sure that we are honoring God in the way we think and live, and that we are not simply being "squeezed into the mold" of the world around us in thought and lifestyle.

2

A Christian mind in everyday life

Should a Christian go to law with another Christian? That was one question before the church at Corinth. It reminds us that the New Testament Epistles were written for people with quite modern problems; for those who, having only recently become Christians, did not automatically find the right answers to their problems. The apostle had frequently to urge them to think toward a solution in truly Christian ways and to bring revealed truths to bear on their lives and on what "seemed right" by instinct. This particular problem, dealt with by Paul in 1 Corinthians 6, produced a most instructive example of Christian thinking for ordinary church members.

"Do you not know. . . ?"

Paul appeals, first of all, to the fact that Christians have a totally different perspective on life through knowledge of revealed truth. Six times in this chapter he says to them, "Do you not know that. . . ?" and in each case he then refers to some revealed Christian truth which, as he goes on to show, helps to solve their problems. Let me quote part of the passage.

> When one of you has a grievance against a brother, does he dare to go to law before the unrighteous instead of the saints?

> *Do you not know* that the saints will judge the world? And if
> the world is to be judged by you, are you incompetent to try
> trivial cases? *Do you not know* that we are to judge angels?
> How much more, matters pertaining to this life! If then you
> have such cases, why do you lay them before those who are
> least esteemed by the church? I say this to your shame. Can it
> be that there is no man among you wise enough to decide
> between members of the brotherhood, but brother goest to
> law against brother, and that before unbelievers? (vv. 1–6).

The apostle then generalizes the point and applies it to other
areas of life:

> To have lawsuits at all with one another is defeat for you.
> Why not rather suffer wrong? Why not rather be defrauded?
> But you yourselves wrong and defraud, and that even your
> own brethren. *Do you not know* that the unrighteous will not
> inherit the kingdom of God? (vv. 7–9).

Here is a typical piece of New Testament writing, and we
can learn a great deal from its method. The apparently purely
practical problem, "Should we go to law with one another?" is
dealt with, not with a simple yes or no, but with a reminder of
some of the great truths of eternity and of salvation taught
explicitly by Jesus Christ (see Matt. 19:28; Luke 22:30; Matt.
24:38–42). Then the Christians are shown how these truths bear
on their attitudes to one another and to their possessions, and so
on the main question at issue. Paul does not actually say that
Christians should never go to law with Christians. He simply
makes it seem ridiculous. The fact that they had such lawsuits at
all, he says, shows that their outlook was wrong. They did not
understand the position of the Christian in God's world, nor had
they the right attitude to fellow Christians or to earthly
possessions. What they needed was not a new rule but a whole
new perspective on life. Truths about the life to come have
practical consequences for this life.

The point is generalized still further in the verses that
follow:

> Do not be deceived; neither the immoral, nor idolaters, nor
> adulterers, nor sexual perverts, nor thieves, nor the greedy,

nor drunkards, nor revilers, nor robbers will inherit the kingdom of God. And such were some of you. But you were washed, you were sanctified (vv. 9–11).

Plainly many of them had been living thoroughly disgraceful lives before they became Christians. It was not enough to say "Don't." A radical rethinking was needed. The whole of life had to come under the criticism of their new understanding of God and of the world, and to be set in a new direction. This was to start by remembering revealed truth and then applying it to their life and outlook. He then concludes, "Do you not know that your body is a temple of the Holy Spirit?" (v. 19).

Paul had lived and taught in Corinth for eighteen months, so the Corinthians had a good background of apostolic teaching. That may be why he can so repeatedly say to them, "Do you not know?" The phrase comes ten times in this letter, far more than in any other, and seems to carry an element of reproof—"Surely you ought to have known."

Paul's method

The point is this, however. To solve some day-to-day practical problems of personal or church life Paul appeals first of all to theological truths that we today might think quite out of this world. Probably none of us would have thought of the fact that "we shall judge angels" as being the most relevant idea to bring to bear on the question of lawsuits. Part of Paul's apostolic wisdom, however, was to show how great truths that may seem quite theoretical do—or should—control our decisions about very mundane issues. Hence one of his characteristic phrases is, "I would have you know," or "We know," or "I remind you" (Peter uses "I intend always to remind you of these things"), and the "Do you not know?" of this passage. These refer to some matters of revealed truth which we need to know if we are to please God in *practice*. Often, as here, they refer to the teaching of Christ or to some explicit Old Testament passage.[1]

---

[1] Just occasionally, they might refer to a matter of common observation as in Romans 6:16, though even here it may well be a reference to our Lord's teaching

For the same reason, Paul, in praying for the churches, gives a big place to praying that they will grow in knowledge (Eph. 1:18–19; Col. 1:9–10). If they did not know the truth in a real way, they could not apply it; and the result would be serious failures of life and witness. As I hope to show, this operates just as much on a practical level as it does on a learned academic level. Indeed, it is sometimes the plain man and woman who find it easiest to put it into practice when the philosophically minded kill it off with a thousand qualifications.

In the New Testament, the Christian mind or renewed mind is a concept used chiefly to help us see how revealed truths impinge on *practical living*. It is not an appeal to be intellectual but rather to be consistent, an encouragement to be adults and not children. Peter, who was not the greatest intellect of the New Testament, speaks in this way when he urges us:

"Therefore gird up your *minds*, be sober, set your hope fully upon the grace that is coming to you at the revelation of Jesus Christ. As obedient children, *do not be conformed* to the passions of your former ignorance, but as he who called you is holy, *be holy yourselves in all your conduct*; since it is written 'You shall be holy, for I am holy' " (1 Peter 1:13–15).

The way in which the New Testament speaks of the Christian mind in the field of conduct or ethics is a guide to what it is intended to be in other areas of life which Scripture does not deal with so explicitly or frequently. For example, our study of the New Testament will tell us whether, in the realm of Christian behavior, we are given a complete set of rules or just a few broad, general principles which we are to apply as best as we can to the practical problems cropping up in our own lives. What we discover in this very carefully developed field can then guide us in other areas.

---

in Matthew 6, "No man can serve two masters." As the following verse (17) says, "You who were once slaves of sin have become obedient from the heart to the *standard* [or pattern] *of teaching* to which you were committed."

The hinge

The idea of a Christian mind comes often in the Epistles, in what can be called the "hinge section," that is to say the section between the more doctrinal part of the epistle and the more practical. Several of the Epistles have a clear structure of this kind. First, there is a short general statement of the aims of the epistle or of the Christian faith as a whole and of what Paul is praying for that church. Then there is a rather long section that explains and develops some of the great themes of personal salvation—the gospel of the grace of God in Jesus Christ. There is then a shorter hinge section that shows *how* these must bear on us in our life. This section usually develops topics such as putting off the old man and putting on the new man, being "in Christ," or being "crucified with Christ." This hinge section then leads on to a final longer part of the epistle in which the Christian life is set out in more practical detail. This is usually done in relation first to personal character and then to the family, the church, and sometimes the state. It is the method Paul uses on a smaller scale when dealing with a particular problem such as rivalry in the church in 1 Corinthians 1–4. In Philippians 2 the doctrinal teaching follows the command to have a Christian mind. The doctrine is a *reason* for having the new attitude. The method is the same even when the order is different.

The point for us is that the theme of the renewed mind comes in the hinge section.[2] It leads *from* doctrine *to* practice and goes on immediately to an outworking in more detailed terms of what it means in daily life. A Christian mind will bear on other aspects of being a Christian, as I hope to show, but it usually relates directly to conduct. It is so well worked out in terms of conduct (or ethics) that this is the best place to start if we want to see what, in practice, the New Testament means by it. This is important, because it is all too easy to use biblical

---

[2] See Romans 12:1–2; Ephesians 4:1–24; 1 Peter 1:13–21; Colossians 3:1–4, and, less clearly perhaps, Philippians 2:1–11; 2 Corinthians 6:1–13. See also Hebrews 10:19–12:4 (where Heb. 11 provides the illustrations). The hinge usually starts with "Therefore."

concepts and phrases like this in unbiblical ways and so to misunderstand their application to us.

Christian ethics

How, then, does a Christian mind work out in the field of ethics? Probably the dearest example is found in Ephesians 4–6. Ephesians 4:1–24 is the hinge section. In these verses Paul uses several arguments of a general kind to persuade us that we must seek with all our energies to lead a consistent life. It starts:

> I therefore [i.e.—in view of all the doctrinal teaching of chapters 1–3], a prisoner for the Lord, beg you to lead a life worthy of the calling to which you have been called, with all lowliness and meekness, with patience, forbearing one another in love, eager to maintain the unity of the Spirit in the bond of peace (vv. 1–3).

Now the usual translations hide the fact that the word translated "lowliness" is more literally translated "lowliness of mind." His first word, therefore, appeals to us to have a new mind about ourselves. Understanding the gospel should give us a totally new attitude to ourselves. In the last part of the hinge section (vv. 17–24) he develops the picture of the mind of the Christian by contrast with the mind that they had had as non-Christians. The passage runs like this:

> Now this I affirm and testify in the Lord, that you must no longer live as the Gentiles do, in the futility of their *minds*; they are darkened in their *understanding*, alienated from the life of God because of the *ignorance* that is in them, due to their hardness of *heart*; they have become callous and have given themselves up to licentiousness, greedy to practice every kind of uncleanness. You did not so *learn* Christ!— assuming that you have *heard* about him and were *taught* in him, as the *truth* is in Jesus (vv. 17–21).

Note the words "minds," "understanding," and "hardness of heart." Paul says that the non-Christians have given themselves up to all kinds of evil as a result of this state of mind and heart. It is probably best to regard verse 17 as the general statement (live in the futility of their minds) and verses 18–19 as an explanation of it. Then verse 20 is a statement of the contrasting Christian position (you learned Christ) and verses 21–24 an explanation of that. So Paul goes on immediately, "You did not so *learn* Christ! . . .you were *taught. . .truth.*"

> You were taught, with regard to your former way of life, to put off your old self, which is being corrupted by its deceitful desires; to be made new [or renewed] in the *attitude of your minds;* and to put on the new self, created to be like God in true righteousness and holiness (vv. 22–24).[3]

A wrong mind in the one case and a right mind in the other are key aspects of the difference between the Christian and the non-Christian. The non-Christian is *ignorant* and the Christian has *learned truth* as it is in Jesus. The non-Christian suffers from *hardness of heart;* the Christian has put off an old *nature* and put on a new one. The non-Christian has a *futile mind;* the Christian has to be renewed in the *spirit of his mind.* If we put this in terms of our Lord's statement of the great commandment, we could say that the Christian has a new *heart* and *mind* because he has by God's grace learned truth as it is in Jesus. A further grammatical point is in order here. Whereas the "put off" and "put on" are in a tense (aorist) which normally signifies a completed process or action, the "be made new in the attitude of your minds" (or RSV, more literally, "be renewed in the spirit of your minds") is a *present* imperative implying that, although we have been given a new nature by new birth ("if any one is in Christ, he is a new creation," 2 Cor. 5:17), the renewal of the

---

[3] I follow the NIV here in verses 22–24. The RSV, for no sufficient reason, follows the AV in translating indicative verbs as if they were *imperatives* ("put on, "put off"). Since the parallel passages in Colossians and Romans 6 state that this putting off and putting on (or dying and rising again) are for the Christian something that happened at conversion, and other passages confirm this, it seems clear that the indicatives must be translated as indicatives. The "to put on" and "to put off" are also indicative aorists—a tense which normally denotes a completed act, not an ongoing process. See the full treatment by John Stott in *God's New Society* (InterVarsity Press, 1979) and H. C. G. Moule, *Ephesians* (Cambridge University Press, 1886).

mind is an *ongoing* process, which is not yet complete, but must be pursued energetically by the Christian.

Now at this point we might have expected Paul to proceed to a general exhortation in terms of love for God and man, to develop, for example, what it means to be recreated in the likeness of God in rather devotional terms, or to say something on the need to imitate Christ. On the contrary, he launches out into a series of hard-hitting practical commands. "Therefore," i.e., because you have a new heart and are being renewed in mind, "putting away falsehood, let everyone *speak the truth.* . . . Do not let the sun go down on your *anger.* . . . Let the thief no longer *steal*, but rather let him labor. . . . Let no *evil talk* come out of your mouths, but only such as is good for edifying." "*Do not get drunk* with wine, . . .but be filled with the Spirit." "Be subject to one another out of reverence for Christ." (This is applied to the *marriage* relationship.) "Children, *obey your parents* in the Lord. . . . Fathers, do not provoke your children to anger. . . . Slaves . . . *rendering service* with a good will. . . . Masters, do the same to them." The other elements, such as imitation of Christ and the need to do these things in love because of God's love for us, are interwoven in 5:1, 2. "Therefore be imitators of God, as beloved children. And walk in love, as Christ loved us and gave himself up for us, a fragrant offering and sacrifice to God." The main thrust of the passage, however, is in terms of a rather precise practical outworking of the Christian life. Imitating God and walking in love are not vague concepts but are seen as having this very practical shape.

Now what can we learn from the fact that the "renewed spirit of your mind" is so suddenly translated into this kind of brisk, hard-hitting ethical exhortation? First of all, the renewal of the mind is essential to sanctification. Without it our daily life will fall far short of what pleases God. Secondly, Paul does not simply say, "Love God and do what you like." He sees that love needs to be guided by commands. There is a school of thought today (usually called "situationalism") which says that the only rule is love and that the Christian will find a sort of built-in homing device that will enable him to discern in every situation what it means to love. The argument is that any alternative will lead to legalism, and we must avoid legalism at all costs. Almost anything, therefore, might be the expression of love. Joseph Gletcher, one of the chief advocates of this school, gives examples to illustrate his belief that, for instance, adultery can be justified in certain circumstances if done in love.[4]

The New Testament shows no sympathy with this outlook, and those who maintain it have to fly in the face of the hard-hitting commands of the New Testament. Our Lord and the New Testament writers clearly do not share such a view. Jesus himself says, "If you love me, you will keep my commandments" (John 14:15). The modern situationalist position is attractive partly because, in the minds of those who advocate it, the only alternative seems to be legalism—a resort to a mere set of rules as a sufficient guide to life. But this is not so.

Love has a shape

Paul was no situationalist. But of all people, Paul is hard to charge with legalism. He spent a large part of his energies, when he was writing the Epistles, in combating legalism in the church (see Galatians and Colossians) and in showing people first that the law is no way to get to heaven, and second, that insisting on the need to keep the full Jewish law is a fundamental denial of the Christian position. Those who think Paul is inconsistent with himself for including these detailed commands in his Epistles have simply fallen into the situationalist false antithesis. Paul at the same time fought legalism and issued ethical commands, as Jesus had done in the Sermon on the Mount. These points are argued out at length and repeatedly.

Paul does not hesitate, therefore, to give us many practical commands, as in Ephesians 4–6. Does he then simply substitute a new kind of law or set of rules for the Old Testament rules? Quite evidently not. If we examine in more detail the kind of thing that he gives us in Ephesians 4–6, we see that he is doing

---

[4]In his book *Situation Ethics* (Westminster, 1967), pp. 164–65. See also J. A. T. Robinson, *Honest to God* (Westminster, 1963), chapter 6, "The New Morality."

something quite different. What he has done is to take a structure provided largely, if not entirely, by the Ten Commandments and then to handle it in a way that is fundamentally following the example of Jesus Christ in the Sermon on the Mount. Jesus there expounded some of the Ten Commandments so as to stress the inner attitudes that they are to represent. "Thou shalt do no murder" means also, he said, that we are not to hate our brother. "Thou shalt not commit adultery" means that we must not think adulterously. "Thou shalt not bear false witness" implies that our words shall always be truthful; our yes must be yes, and our no, no.

Paul here does not mention the command, "Thou shalt do no murder," but develops the theme of anger and hatred of our neighbors in very much the same way our Lord did in Matthew 5. Ephesians 4 has here, "Be angry but do not sin; do not let the sun go down on your anger, and give no opportunity to the devil." When it comes to stealing (in the Old Testament "Thou shalt not steal"), Paul here says, "Let the thief no longer steal, but rather let him labor, doing honest work with his hands, so that he may be able to give to those in need. He takes the negative commandment about stealing, reaffirms it, and then puts it in the context of the positive Christian ideal of an alternative—seeking to put something back into society and to meet the needs of others, rather than being a parasite. Coveting (the tenth commandment) he refers to as idolatry (Eph. 5:5). In 5:3–14 he gives the Christian expansion of the seventh commandment, and in 6:1–2 he repeats the fifth commandment. He sets it all, however, in a wider context with "Walk in love, as Christ loved us and gave himself up for us, a fragrant offering and sacrifice to God" (5:2), and he shows how the commandments should be carried out (i.e., nonlegalistically). Paul is offering neither a "Love God and do what you like" view of the Christian life nor a new Christian legalism. He makes it plain that his overall rule is love, but love which is worked out in intelligent application of the known will of God as outlined in the Ten Commandments, understood as Jesus taught us to understand them. The New Testament does not simply reissue the commandments; it uses them somewhat as a framework but sees them in terms of the gospel of liberty.

What, then, is Paul giving us in the way of a Christian mind in ethics? Perhaps the most concise answer is to say that he emphasizes a new spirit and gives us a structured ethic. If that sounds rigid, it may be better to call it a principled ethic. He provides us with a framework for our living which consists, first, of some general principles—walk in love, speak the truth, do honest work, etc., and also some particular fixed points which show us what the general things mean: "Be sure of this, that no fornicator or impure man, or one who is covetous (that is an idolater), has any inheritance in the kingdom of Christ and of God" (5:5). It is not a new legalism, but a life ruled by love of God and love of men, in harmony with the structure of the revealed truth that God had given (love of his commandments). It is part of a whole Christian *outlook* in which we hate whatever we know God hates and love what he loves. What that should mean in practice has, however, been made known to us in outline.

We have, therefore, not a new rule-book, but a whole approach to practical living based on the things God has been pleased to tell us—theological truths, ethical truth and a few fixed points where God has treated us still as children who need a "thou shalt" and "thou shalt not." These few fixed points provide some examples and illustrations of what it means to have a Christian mind in ethics. There are other well-worked examples in Bible history and biography (e.g., David), and in the New Testament some complex issues are discussed at length, such as meat offered to idols, and marriage. The New Testament certainly transforms Old Testament ethics, but the metamorphosis leaves its essentials the same, the Sermon on the Mount being our pattern here.[5]

We are warned by our Lord in the Sermon on the Mount never to think that keeping the specifics is the whole of our duty.

---

[5] For a fuller discussion see my essay on "The Nature of Christian Morality" in *Law, Morality and the Bible*, ed. B. N. Kaye and G. J. Wenham (InterVarsity Press, 1978).

Our righteousness must be far more than that. Matthew 5:20 tells us that "unless your righteousness exceeds that of the scribes and Pharisees, you will never enter 'the kingdom of heaven.'" Our life must be the fruit of a new heart and a renewed mind—a whole renewed inner spirit and outlook on life. It is far from legalism but it is not unstructured. *Love has a shape* in the New Testament.

The starting point

The New Testament mind about conduct is also not what is called "praxis" theology. This phrase usually means that we start with a sociological or similar analysis of the actual situation and look at our theological framework in the light of that analysis. I would be bold to say that there is no trace of this approach in the New Testament. In fact, as I showed in the relation to going to law, Paul's methodology is exactly the opposite. He tells us to remember first the great revealed truths, not to work first at the human theories about how societies function. "Do you not know. . . ?" is followed by theological statements, not economic, scientific, psychological, or sociological ones. We can be thankful to these praxis theologians if they ask us to bring radical criticism to bear on how our theology works in practice in society and in our own lives. But the method they advocate is not the New Testament method. It is true that our Lord said, "You will know them by their fruits" (Matt. 7:16). This we must face. But we must follow the method of the New Testament if we are to arrive at a truly Christian way of developing a Christian life.

In 1 Corinthians 7–9 there is a discussion about marriage and meat offered to idols. Here Paul's approach is basically the same. He starts in the first case with a Christian view of the marriage relationship and our Lord's own explicit instructions. In the matter of meat offered to idols he starts with the Christian view of God and of idols ("We *know* that 'an idol has no real existence,' and that 'there is no God but one'") before grappling with the fact that some Christians do not "possess this knowledge" and need to be helped in love. The same "Do you not know?" phrase is used in relation to two other separate problems in 1 Corinthians (church discipline and incest), and similar approaches abound in other New Testament ethical passages (e.g., 2 Cor. 8:9 on giving). Again and again the apostle is working from revealed knowledge of the real nature of the situation, rather than making a sociological study.

In harmony with this the blessing of God is in the Bible promised to those who study and obey God's revelation (see Josh. 1 and Deut. 5–8), not to those who are clever at military strategy (or, today, skilled in business methods) or whose minds are full of the latest knowledge—whatever subsidiary place that may have. It is not that we should despise the use of knowledge from whatever source it comes, if it is true knowledge. Quite the contrary; we want as much knowledge as possible. The point is that the Christian mind is something created essentially by God's revealed Word coming to bear on us so that we think in accordance with that. Thinking in accordance with the latest insights of sociology or medicine or educational psychology is properly called sociology, medicine, or educational theory, and, even if it happens to be true, it is not distinctively Christian. The Christian should be eager to make use of all truths, but do not let us call this modern knowledge the Christian mind. The Christian mind values truth from whatever source it comes, but it involves seeing all of life, including modern knowledge, under the control of God's Word, which is *God's truth* made known to us. Jesus' response to questions about divorce in Matthew 19 is another good example. The diciples started with the hardships created by difficult marriages. Jesus insists on making them start with the creation order: "In the beginning . . . God said. . . ." What makes the Christian mind Christian is its dependence on God's revelations. It will share with non-Christians a respect for any kind of truth (see chapter 5).

Let's take another modern example. In a conference of Christian teachers the problem arose of what to do about pornographic literature that circulated in a particular school. Various possible measures were discussed, and people made suggestions about what should and should not go on in the school. After a while, however, a school administrator got up and described the following program. He said that, looking at the whole problem in what he hoped was a Christian way, he dealt with it by confiscating the literature and then sending it with a letter to the parents. In this letter he explained to them that he did not regard it as his responsibility what the student read at home. That was the parents' responsibility, and he was therefore returning the book to the parents for them to decide whether they wished to take any action. As principal of the school, however, he did have the responsibility of seeing that such literature did not circulate in the school. He asked the parents to please make sure that, whatever was allowed at home, the boy never again brought such material to school.

This solution immediately commended itself to almost everybody present (as indeed it would to many non-Christian teachers). The interesting thing about this, however, is that what this particular administrator had done was to bring to bear on the situation a theological truth which the others had on the whole overlooked. He had recognized that the Christian gives to the authority of parents the primary place in the moral upbringing of their children. He sought by his method to help them do their God-given duty. He was doing it in such a way that he hoped both to strengthen the parental role in education and to gain their cooperation with the school in the whole task of moral education. There are other features of this solution, such as the demarcation of areas of authority, which are interesting; but the point is that he brought to bear on this situation what other people missed, a broader Christian view of who has responsibility for moral education and a whole Christian view of society and its authority structures. Others had overlooked the parents.

The New Testament, therefore, practically never answers an ethical problem with a quick yes or no on the one hand, or with a principle so general that its application is uncertain on the other. Thus, to those who say that Christian ethics must be a matter either of love or of legalism, the New Testament answer is that it is primarily love, but love can be expressed in the Ten Commandments and other ethical principles. In Romans 13, for instance, Paul puts it like this:

Owe no one anything, except to *love* one another; for he who loves his neighbor has fulfilled the law. The *commandments,* "You shall not commit adultery, You shall not kill, You shall not steal, You shall not covet," and any other commandment, are summed up in this sentence, "You shall *love* your neighbor as yourself." Love does no wrong to a neighbor, therefore love is the fulfilling of the law (vv. 8–11).

Note that love fulfills the law and does not ignore or abolish it.[6] The law provides the framework of what it means to love, so that the man who says that in love he kills his handicapped baby, or in love he leaves his wife and goes off with somebody else, has to face the fact that that is not what the New Testament means by love, but a sentimental and unbiblical view of love. J. A. T. Robinson, the former bishop of Woolwich, who was counted among the situationalists, wrote in one place as follows, "Love alone, because, as it were, it has a built-in moral compass, enabling it to 'home' intuitively upon the deepest need of the other, can allow itself to be directed completely by the situation."[7] But love's true goals are not so easy to discover. If we were not fallen and ignorant, what Robinson said could be true; but we are both sinful and also part blind, so God in his goodness gives us guidelines and structures. He does not, however, give us a complete system of rules and regulations. Even the Old Testament law, in all its complexity for a theocratic society, did not provide a complete system. The New Testament, written for people in a great variety of cultures, is much further from a complete system, and those churches that have tried to develop a complete pastoral rule-book have inevitably fallen into legalism, as even the Jews of our Lord's day did in their use of the Old Testament.

This is not the place to develop a full picture of New Testament ethics. There is much more to be said, but I hope I have shown that the Christian mind applied to ethics and to the Christian life in general is something different from both

---

[6] Compare Matthew 5:17–20 where Jesus first taught the principle. He came not to abolish the Law and the Prophets, but to fulfill them. As so often Paul is very close to the words of Christ.

[7] *Honest to God,* p. 115.

situationalism and legalism. Its method, which is the opposite of a praxis approach, is to appeal to revealed truth and to let love be controlled by truth so that it can be applied to particular situations. The revealed truths in question, however, are a framework of principles or a structure which leaves to us the task of responsible decision in areas where Christians have to apply God's instruction to new situations and new issues. It is a creative freedom to live out our Christian faith within the framework, and the New Testament stresses that it is indeed true freedom. Thinking by Christians (however sophisticated) that does not have this absolute anchorage in God's revelation is not truly Christian thinking. As the Book of Common Prayer has it, "His service is perfect freedom."

Paul therefore, as for example in Galatians 5 and 6, can attack legalism and stress love and freedom and, at the same time, also stress that, for the Christian, love and freedom express themselves in certain particular ways, by enabling us to live more nearly as we are created to live. Just because the Christian is ruled by the Spirit of God, he has the mind of the Spirit, shows certain specific fruits of the Spirit, and hates and denies certain specific works of the flesh (see Gal. 5:16–26). We must hold all these together and not try to oversimplify the view of the Christian life in terms of only one or two of these elements such as "freedom in the Spirit," "love," or "commandments." God does not want us to be a series of zombies all acting in an identically programmed way. In Christ we have life, and we have it more abundantly; but that does not mean we can go off and "do our own thing." On the contrary, as Paul puts it in 1 Corinthians 6: "*Do you not know* that your bodies are members of Christ? . . . *Do you not know* that your body is a temple of the Holy Spirit within you? . . . So glorify God in your body." In the course of that passage he is also saying there are certain things that a Christian can never do. We are not left to look inside ourselves for our own compass. We are left to work out our pattern of life and our individual decisions in the light of the love of God and Christ's example and teaching expressed in revealed principles, illustrated by some detailed applications. That is what it is to have a Christian mind in ethics.

3

A Christian mind in doctrine

I have argued that we have a clear presentation in the New Testament of Christian ethics as a structured (or principled) ethic. It is not a legalistic system of rules, on the one hand, or situation ethics, with only one rule, on the other. It is neither hard and brittle (legalism) nor soft and pliable (situationalism), but tough like steel. New Testament morality comes to us as revealed guidelines with the authority of God for our acceptance, but also for careful outworking in our own different situations. It requires a new *heart* of love for God and man, but also requires a *mind* controlled by Scripture and renewed in its whole outlook.

If this is true of ethics, however, what about Christian doctrine? Is Christian doctrine presented to us as a complete system which hangs together in a unity that cannot be breached without grave injury to the whole? Or how can we think of it? This is a vital question. As we have said, Christian ethics depends upon Christian doctrine. We are called upon to remember what to us may be somewhat obscure Christian truths in order to solve very practical questions. If the Christian mind means bringing Christian doctrine to bear on our practical lives and our thinking, we need to be quite clear as to what sort of a thing Christian doctrine is. Is it a series of independent and unrelated truths, or is there a complete network of doctrines that we can identify as "sound doctrine" (the Greek means healthy or healthgiving), so that all alternatives are "unsound" or positively wrong and undermine the health of the church? Alternatively, is it not a system at all, but a personal relationship?

The claim for objective truth

First we must say that, as Christians, we are claiming that there is such a thing as objective revealed truth. Indeed, this is a key aspect of having a Christian mind at all. This is currently not a popular claim. Today we are often told that all beliefs are only a matter of our own *interpretation*. On this view no one interpretation has any more authority than another, unless it be that it is believed by many clever people. We are told that there may be events created by God, such as the incarnation, death, and (perhaps) the resurrection of Christ, but their significance is something for the church to decide. Those decisions as to what is the significance of these events will always be culture-bound and relative. Those who hold this view stress, for instance, that the understanding of the person of Christ which we find in the New Testament documents is only a spiritual *interpretation* of events or of the writers' experience of Christ. Our task, they say, is to demythologize those interpretations and to reinterpret the experience of the New Testament church in our own modern categories.

Our whole culture in the second half of the twentieth century is deeply influenced by various subjective traditions of this kind. This is partly a reaction to excessive claims for human knowledge in the sciences—where we now know that most theories are subject to modification—and to excessive dogmatism in philosophy. We have swung over into a failure of nerve that tries to treat all knowledge as so relative and so subject to the influence of the one who observes or knows that in the end we are left only with opinions. The trends we have mentioned in theology follow the current culture. A shrewd observer, when asked why the subjective tradition in academic theology is popular in some circles, commented, I think rightly, that it is basically because it is so tied to the culture of the late twentieth century! Nowadays it is easier to think like that than to think, as the New Testament does, of objective truth. The only certainties that we are left with on this view are the certainties of subjective experience—"This idea gets me," or "I feel convinced that God is like this," or "I have no doubt that reality is like that." This comes constantly into modern preaching and writing. Even the most orthodox preachers are frequently found to be saying merely, "I believe that. . . ," as if the fact that they believed it had any authority at all and was to the hearers anything more than a psychological curiosity.

Perhaps the situation is best illustrated by the recent reports of the Doctrine Commission of the Church of England. Its first report in 1976 surprised people by its failure to discuss *doctrine* at all. It discussed only how Christians do in fact believe things—not what they believe. Its title, significantly, was *Christian Believing*. Even after considerable criticism of this first report, the second one, published in 1981 by a somewhat different group of people, did exactly the same thing. It was called *Believing in the Church*, and, in spite of its deliberate ambiguity of title, it dealt simply with *how* people in the church believe and did not even mention *what* they believed about the church. This is understandable, however, if you no longer believe that there is such a thing as "the faith once for all delivered to the saints." These reports have a constant confusion between "the faith" and "faith," i.e., between what is believed and the act of believing. But one suspects that many of the authors no longer hold that there is such a thing as the Christian faith capable of being described in any way.

By contrast listen to Paul. In 1 Corinthians 15:3–4, 12–14, and 20–22 he says:

> For I delivered to you as of first importance what I also received, that Christ died for our sins in accordance with the scriptures, that he was buried, that he was raised on the third day in accordance with the scriptures. Now if Christ is preached as raised from the dead, how can some of you say that there is no resurrection of the dead? But if there is no resurrection of the dead, then Christ has not been raised; if Christ has not been raised, then our preaching is in vain and

your faith is in vain. But in fact Christ has been raised from the dead, the first fruits of those who have fallen asleep. For as by a man came death, by a man has come also the resurrection of the dead. For as in Adam all die, so also in Christ shall all be made alive.

First the apostle affirms certain historical facts ("Christ died" and "in fact Christ has been raised from the dead"). Then he says that they mean something ("for our sins") and that they are "according to the scriptures." He then declares certain interpretations and consequences of those facts for our salvation, e.g., "in Christ shall all be made alive." The New Testament apostles clearly believed, not only that God had brought certain things to pass, but also that he had given us the right understanding of those events. The fact of the death of Christ is qualified by "for our sins in accordance with the scriptures." The sense in which his death would be for our sins was clear in the Old Testament Scriptures (see, e.g., Isa. 53); and Paul here (and Peter equally in 1 Peter 2 and John in 1 John 2) affirms that same Old Testament interpretation of the facts as God-given truth. There is no reason to accept the events as God-given and to deny that God has equally given us his meaning (or interpretation) of those facts. The apostles claim the same status for their interpretation as for their witness to the facts. God is equally capable of giving both in accordance with the real state of affairs as he sees it. Either the death of Christ was "for our sins," in the Old Testament sense of that phrase, or it was not. The apostles say that it was. That is a truth about the way things actually are in God's universe as much as is the fact that Christ died on the cross. Either there is or there is not a future physical resurrection for those "in Christ." Jesus and all the New Testament writers say that there is.

There can be no serious doubt that Jesus and his carefully instructed disciples believed and taught that they were passing on to us truth. That is to say, they believed that they were by God's revelation able to tell us things that are in fact the case in God's universe and to express them in words which were expected to convey truth to us. Jesus, for instance, repeatedly made this claim, and so did the apostles (see, e.g., John 1:1–5 and Gal. 1:6–9). Like Jesus (in Mark 13:32–33) the apostles knew that their knowledge was limited and also that certain questions were unanswerable with a yes or no (e.g., in Mark 12:23, "In the resurrection whose wife will she be?" or in 1 Corinthians 7, "Is a man wrong to marry?"). But they did not hesitate to say that those things which were revealed were the truth or "the word of God," as they called it on other occasions.

We sometimes sing rather glibly that

He is Lord,
He is Lord,
He is risen from the dead and he is Lord.
Every knee shall bow,
Every tongue confess
That Jesus Christ is Lord.

This is of course a most controversial statement about the afterlife. How can Christians say that? The answer is that they can do so only because God has been kind enough to tell us that it is true. Biblical Christianity is absolutely committed to the fact that *God has spoken* and has spoken to tell us what is the case so that we may respond to truth and not merely to opinion. To sing that chorus can be a joyful act of worship, but only because we know the truths that lead us to worship.

How complete is the revelation?

Our *formulations* of revealed truth are, of course, not infallible. Our scientific understanding of the physical world is also imperfect, but it does enable us to build reliable bridges, airplanes, and computers. It is sufficiently near to the actual state of affairs in God's world for us to rely on its outworking.

The New Testament doctrine of revelation is that God has given us *sufficient* revealed knowledge to live by. In 2 Timothy 3:1–9, Paul describes the chaotic situation that was to arise shortly in the church. People claiming to be believers would teach all sorts of heresies and ethical errors. What is Timothy to do in this situation? The answer in verses 13–18 is that, although "evil men and impostors will go on from bad to worse," Timothy is to go back to "what you have learned and have firmly believed, knowing from whom you learned it" (i.e., from the apostles).[1] Paul goes on, "and how from childhood you have been acquainted with the sacred writings" (i.e., the Old Testament). For, he says, "all scripture is inspired by God . . . that the man of God may be complete, equipped for every good work."

He does not here, or anywhere else, say that God has revealed everything. As Jesus particularly said, he has not revealed the date of the Second Coming. What he does say is that God has "breathed out"[2] the Scriptures so that men may have *enough* for the whole Christian life. The Scriptures are sufficient; and even though poetic insight, psychology, sociology, and Christian philosophy can be useful in some circumstances, we do not need them to be "complete, equipped for every good work."

Here, also, Paul makes plain the aim of revelation. It is not given just to satisfy our intellectual curiosity. It is not given to be a philosophical system for its own sake. It is given so that, in the life both of the church and of the individual, we have enough to go on to live a life pleasing to God and to avoid the errors that matter. It is "for teaching, for reproof, for correction, and for training in righteousness" (v. 16). Its purpose is not to make the man of God complete for other interesting, but relatively unimportant, purposes, even if, like a precise economic theory

[1] Those people who want this to refer to Timothy's Jewish mother and grandmother, who had both become Christians, have surely failed to notice the context. Could Paul possibly say, "When the whole church is in danger consult the view of a recently converted Jewish grandmother and mother (married to a Gentile, which shows that she was not even a strict Jew) and you will know the answers"? Perhaps the mother and grandmother taught him to read the Old Testament, but that is Paul's next point.

[2] When an important church leader said (or is reported to have said) at the Church of England Synod in July 1982 that the concept of inspiration of the Bible was "too general and vague to be of value" because Beethoven and T. S. Eliot were also inspired, he forgot that the Bible word translated "inspired" is literally "god-breathed"—"ex-spired" rather than "in-spired." That is a total different concept from musical or literary "inspiration."

for today or the principles of physical or psychological health, they are things that our culture leads us to value.

What kind of doctrinal system?

Are we then given a complete doctrinal system? The first answer to this question, as we have seen already, is that we are given truths—those truths that God wants us to know so that we may live by them. But do these truths form a system or not? Is there a coherent biblical theology/philosophy which we can spell out and put in writing for our own generation? The answer I am suggesting is that in doctrine, as in ethics, we have a framework but not a complete system. In the Bible, Christian doctrine forms a structured theology. We have a framework of particular truths that fit together and are interrelated, and not just a collection of unrelated truths. There is a unifying theme, but there is more than one separate strand. There are three main arguments for this standpoint.

Christ, the Truth

First, the truth in the New Testament is repeatedly spoken of as expressed, not in a system, but in a person—the person of Jesus. He said, "I am the truth." Paul, when writing in Ephesians about the Christian mind, talks, as we have seen, about "the truth as it is in Jesus." He does not say, "the truth as it is expressed in my system." Other passages emphasize the same fact. Hebrews 1:1–4, for instance, stresses that, although in the past God spoke by the prophets "in many and various ways," "in these last days he has spoken to us by a Son." Here is a deliberate contrast between the *truths* that were given in time past to the prophets (and that of course emphasizes their value and reliability) and the fuller and finally complete revelation in a different form. The new form of truth is a person, Jesus Christ himself, not just a new intellectual theological scheme. The capstone of Christian theology is not a key idea or notion. It is Jesus himself who is the headstone of the corner. We shall therefore search in vain, and are likely sadly to distort the truth, if we look for its unity in something like a philosophical system or the theological equivalent of some key scientific concept that unifies a great deal of knowledge. The unity of Christian revelation is in Christ, not in a theological system.

This has very far-reaching consequences. It means that Christian doctrine is different from a mere assembly of truths, however well put together. Christian doctrine has a new dimension. Our knowledge of God and man and salvation and eternity is not to be thought of as less than embodied in the person of Jesus Christ. The passage in 1 Corinthians 1, which we discussed earlier and which deals with human wisdom and divine wisdom, comes to a close in these words: "Christ Jesus, whom God made our wisdom, our righteousness and sanctification and redemption; therefore as it is written, 'Let him who boasts, boast *of the Lord.*' "

One amazing result of this, for which we must all be deeply thankful, is that we do not have to be clever to have a profound faith. Even a simple child can have the heart of the matter and can have grasped the unifying theme of all theology, ethics, and philosophy, because he can have a personal faith in Jesus Christ as the one who is above all and "in whom are hid all the treasures of wisdom and knowledge" (Col. 2:3). Thus Jesus said: "I praise you, Father, Lord of heaven and earth, because you have hidden these things from the wise and learned, and revealed them to little children. Yes, Father, for this was your good pleasure" (Matt 11:25–26, NIV).

Revealed truths

Second however, there is *a wide range of teaching* (doctrines or truths) in addition to what obviously fits under this heading. The passage we have just considered in Hebrews 1:1–4 makes it plain that there are truths of Old Testament revelation. They are unified and caught up in the one great revelation in Christ; but they are also, in their own right, truths of God's *Word*—"In the past God *spoke."* It is all too easy to make the entirely correct emphasis on the unity of truth that is in Christ an excuse for downgrading those clear teachings of the Bible that Jesus and his disciples in fact affirmed. We must, for instance, allow the Old Testament teaching of God as Creator and as Lord of history to stand even before we have seen the relationship of that teaching to Christ as the agent of creation and the Lord of time. There are doctrines that relate primarily to the truth of God as Father and Creator, and others that relate primarily to the truth of God the Holy Spirit, even though they all relate also to God the Son.

Those who want to maintain that everything is adequately summarized in speaking of "the truth as it is in Jesus" are sometimes (not always) found to be using this to avoid other biblical teaching. The result can be a doctrinally shapeless Christianity, parallel to the shapeless view of "love" which we have noted in ethics. At least it has led to a Christianity whose shape can be readily molded to serve the particular favorite emphasis of different theologians.

This view could be called the doctrinal equivalent of situationalism in ethics. We must never forget that Jesus is the supreme expression of truth, and that all truth is united in Him, just as we must not forget that love is the supreme expression of Christian ethics. But God in his goodness has given us also particular truths. To state this is not to downgrade Jesus, any more than to say that there are ethical truths is to downgrade love as the paramount ethical principle. We must accept the way the Bible gives us truths. Both situationalist ethics and the attempt to state all doctrine in terms of "Jesus only" owe much, in fact, to the existentialist mood of our day and sometimes to sophisticated existentialist thinking. They may be part of our secular culture, but we are aiming to be biblical Christians, not merely modern men and women.

An incomplete system

Third, the Bible nowhere gives us a complete system. If a fully worked out system of doctrine were what we needed, then we would presumably have been given it in the Bible. Indeed, the very fact that it has not been given to us warns us that there are dangers inherent in too much reliance on systematization. The New Testament speaks of "the *pattern* of the sound words" (2 Tim. 1:13). Paul in Romans 6:17 talks of being "obedient from the heart to the standard [or *pattern*] of *teaching* to which you were committed." (The Jerusalem Bible translation of "pattern of teaching" as "creeds" is an anachronism and an oversimplification, but is not altogether misleading.) Both passages stress that this pattern is there for us to follow and obey. The truths are to control our minds and our lives. These and similar phrases clearly indicate that the truths do fit together and form a unity. The word used in 2 Timothy 1 and Romans 6 for "pattern" or "standard" means not a complete picture but an outline sketch for others to fill in. The particular truths of the New Testament form just such an incomplete pattern, and, as a result, they relate to one another and to some extent depend upon one another. In some respects the modern word "network" corresponds to the biblical word "pattern." In a net, a break at one point will tend to spread more and more widely. Especially when it is under tension, the net will be distorted in its shape and function if even only one strand breaks. The effect of that break will be greater on the other threads that are nearest to it. You see the same in a spider's web when one strand breaks.

Christian doctrine is rather like such a net. If you deny one of the major strands of truth it soon begins to affect the rest, starting with those truths that lie nearest to it. Deny, for instance, the deity of Christ, and if we are at all consistent in our thinking, the nature of his death is immediately altered. Next the authority of his ethical teaching goes. Finally the view of the nature of the church is undermined so that, within a generation or so, even the church loses its authority and cannot hold together what was once held together by faith in the divine Savior. Or again, to start with a less fundamental truth; if we teach that the human body is in itself evil, this error works outward toward other doctrines and has historically resulted either in a false asceticism or (as in the Gnostic tradition) in the view that sin performed in the body does not really matter. But that turns much of the New Testament on its head. Righteous living obviously matters intensely. An apparently remote error has worked through to an area where it is obviously wrong. There is in the New Testament a pattern of interrelated truths which reinforce and clarify one another, and we are to make sure that our *mind* and *heart* are controlled by this pattern. We can allow the use of the word "system" to describe this, so long as it is made clear that it is an incomplete system.

Recently I saw an article in which the author attacked all idea of a systematic theology. He claimed, quite correctly, that our system is in Christ and his person. He went on, however, to say that the whole idea of a system "starting with sin and justification and going on to sanctification and glorification" owed more to books of systematic theology than to the New Testament and should be abandoned. We should, he said, just preach Christ and him crucified and not have any system beyond that.

The short answer to this is to say that, in fact, the Epistle to the Romans was written before the books of systematic theology which our friend criticized—a long while before! If we ask why Romans is a much more systematic setting out of doctrine than the other Epistles, there are some obvious reasons. Paul had never visited Rome. In Corinth and Ephesus he had lived and taught for more than a year not too long before he wrote his letters. In other Epistles he was dealing with particular needs of people he knew and had taught, at least for a short time. Of Paul's Epistles, only Romans and Colossians are explicitly written to people who had never had the advantage of a basic groundwork teaching period from the apostle himself. Colossians is strikingly systematic in a different way, but Paul was in that letter also dealing with a special problem (as in Galatians and Philippians). Only in Romans does he seem to have been at liberty to give an outline of the gospel and its implications that was relatively free from the constraints of an urgent need to refute particular errors or moral faults, though he does of course address himself to a number of disputed issues on the way through, such as the relation of Jew and Gentile.

In any case, here (and in Colossians) he does provide us with an outline that is more systematic. Yes, there is a pattern of doctrines that holds together, but it is not presented to us in anything like a complete system such as might be needed in a textbook of systematic theology.

This does not mean that to write such a systematic theology is an improper task. On the contrary, there is great value in working out how the basic framework of New Testament doctrine leads us into a clear understanding of biblical teaching in more detailed areas. The Old Testament background, for instance, may clarify and confirm New Testament teaching where it may be compressed into a few phrases that would be ambiguous without the Old Testament context. Consider, for example, the meaning of the phrase "lamb of God" and its bearing on the doctrine of the atonement.

Romans, for instance, does not include a systematic setting out of the doctrine of man, though many elements of it are there. Indeed, no particular New Testament passage in itself sets this out systematically. It is evident, however, that the main outlines of a doctrine of man are referred to in different places, so that we can see that Christians were not in doubt about its chief features. There is value, therefore, in trying to spell it out systematically by inference from the teaching that we do have. At the very least it saves us the work of starting from scratch every time a new issue arises that involves this doctrine. Indeed, in today's climate, a grasp of the outline of Christian doctrine is more than ever important. Christians sometimes come up with the most naive and unbiblical teaching because they have failed to see that it is inconsistent with other things that are clearly taught in the Bible. Those who want us to preach "only Christ" in the sense I have mentioned must be aware of how that has allowed some bizarre and unbiblical teaching when it has not been held alongside an emphasis both on the particular biblical truths and on an understanding of how they fit together.

To look at one example, some people have stated that Paul may have changed his teaching about the Second Coming in the course of his life, so that he later repudiated views that he held earlier. Some of these writers are shocked when they discover the implications of that view. They do not at first see that, in that case, we are faced with the task of choosing between the earlier and the later Paul as an authoritative apostle. They usually assume the later Paul was right and the earlier mistaken. The earlier Paul, however, is more likely to have been closer to the teaching of Christ. If the earlier Paul is mistaken, does that mean that Christ was mistaken? If Christ was mistaken about this, in what other doctrines was he mistaken? If, on the other hand, the later Paul was mistaken, then how many of the other "developed" doctrines taught by Paul were also mistaken? The chain effect of an error, which some of those concerned have now retracted, was not realized until they did a little more thinking about the systematic (network) aspects of doctrine.

Can we create a systematic theology?

We have to face the fact, however, that, when people have set out to erect a *complete* systematic theology that is based on the Bible, they have not always ended up with exactly the same result. There is massive agreement on the main points; but there are also some differences both of emphasis and of substance in some areas. Can we be certain which one is right or are all of them equally in error? There are a Reformed (Calvinistic), a Lutheran, a Methodist, an Anglican, a Baptist, a Charismatic, and a Brethren system of Christian doctrine, and they are not identical. The task of creating a biblical outline of interrelated doctrine is obviously not as simple as it seems. How do we explain the situation?

Granted that, if we accept the authority of the Bible, then there is a very large area of agreement and many agreed statements of particular doctrines, how is it that we put them together differently? The answer is probably obvious. First, we are talking about God. We have great difficulty in science in arriving at agreed statements about some aspects of the physical world. How much more are we bound to find difficulty in talking about God! It is true that we can be sure of certain scientific facts and we can be sure of certain theological truths because they are so widely based on such a variety of data (scientific or biblical, as the case may be). But in theology we are acutely aware that we are trying to describe things too big for the human mind. If God has revealed his holiness, his love and grace, and his sovereignty, then we will hold those things with assurance, but we are bound to confess that they are only a small part of God's character and that we cannot comprehend the whole. We can cope only with what God has been pleased to reveal. We must never forget the element of mystery and awe in front of the living God, even when he has made aspects of the truth quite plain to us. No theologian is big enough to hold all in a perfect relationship.

Second, every systematizer of theology has to (or at least ought to) admit that there are some biblical passages and some biblical truths that do not fit altogether comfortably into his system. The system tries to cope with all the data, but it is not a perfect fit at some points.

Third, all such systems are a kind of shortcut. Lacking explicit biblical teaching in some areas, we have filled in the gaps with what seemed to be convincing deductions from those things that are quite clear. The result has the strengths and weaknesses of any shortcut. It enables us to cover the ground without endless hesitation and complications, but it is leaving the sure ground of a well-marked path for unmapped territory. In the course of time a shortcut may be well marked also, but it is not on the map and involves some measure of departure from certainty.

We find ourselves like a man flying over the Alps on a cloudy day. He is able to see all the peaks, but if there is a belt of cloud at 2,000 meters he can often not see how the separate mountains relate to one another or what the terrain in between is like. Nevertheless he can see enough to know exactly where to fly and where not to fly! He has no doubt about that. It is only when he comes below the level of clear visibility that he has to work out from his experience in other mountain chains where the valleys are likely to be, and here he has to rely on radar rather than vision or guesswork. His guesses are often wrong.

We are confronted with alternative systems of biblical theology, and each copes better with some aspects of biblical teaching and with some aspects of life and thought than the others. Historically, for instance, the Calvinistic system has coped best of all with the world of culture, politics, education, science, and philosophy. It has had its weak points, however, in some areas. Compared with the Methodist and Brethren traditions, it has probably more often allowed weakness in missionary enthusiasm. That is not a necessary weakness. When people in this tradition are well and constantly fed with a wide reading and exposition of the Bible, then this system, like the others, is preserved from the weaknesses to which it is most open and has retained the beauty of a faith that is truly Christ-centered. Those in the Reformed tradition, however, who think they have nothing biblical to learn from the Methodist and Pietist traditions are sadly blind—and vice versa.

Every system has at times been in danger of taking the place that belongs to the essential personal faith in and devotion to Christ. That is not a reason for avoiding a system. Indeed, we must systematize our faith to some extent if we are to think as Christians at all and if we are to have the tools to grapple with particular situations without enormous labor. A system is an almost necessary shortcut, and as we have seen, the Bible itself systematizes doctrine to some extent and clearly envisages a pattern.

Is all doctrine uncertain?

Certainly the doubt about the adequacy of any one complete system and the fact that the Bible does not set out a full systematic theology must not lead us to believe that all Christian doctrine is only tentative and uncertain. If God has spoken in such a way that he gives us words and concepts that we ourselves can use to describe his person and work, we are not only timid but disloyal if we refuse to use them. To take an obvious example: if the Bible says both that God is love and that he is holy (and it does), it is not intellectual modesty but pride which would lead us to refuse to state both and to preach both with confidence, even if the relation between the two is not fully resolved in our little minds. Or again, if man cannot save himself by any moral or religious activity, is totally dead spiritually, and can be saved only by the entirely undeserved mercy of God, then we must say so, even if we are not so confident as to how these truths relate to the call for a human response to the gospel. The truth about God may even seem paradoxical to us.

To return to the analogy of the man flying over the Alps: the fact that we did not see the whole picture must not lead us to assume that we have not been shown some of it so clearly that we have more than enough to go on to steer our thinking and our living. We must affirm with confidence what is given us clearly. These considerations lead us to insist on a distinction between, on the one hand, those truths that are beyond doubt the teaching of the Bible and, on the other hand, those that are inferences from those truths or from less clear Bible statements. The latter may be very compelling inferences which we personally cannot doubt. But this is where Oliver Cromwell's plea to the Church of Scotland comes in. "I beseech you, in the bowels of Christ, think it possible you may be mistaken." He was talking about the way they worked out their (mutually agreed) faith into areas of practical politics. We must avoid the temptation to affirm these conclusions based on inference from biblical truth as if they were as certain as those things clearly and unequivocally taught in the Bible. The lust for intellectual tidiness must be resisted when it leads us to dogmatize about what is not clear in Scripture.

If we do not make such a distinction, one or both of two results follows. We may become known chiefly for things that are really incidental to what the Bible regards as important but which happen to be controversial or of interest to society. Our political stance, for instance, may become the chief thing by which we are recognized, or our views on pacificism, drink, baptism, the date of the Second Coming, church leadership, or charismatic gifts. And we may fall into the trap of regarding all truths as of equal importance, so that we dismiss as heretics those who do not share every detail of our system. This is clearly not the New Testament position. Paul is constantly urging Christians of somewhat different views and somewhat different practice to be of one mind and to work together because they hold the essentials of the Christian faith and life in common. It is as vital today as it was then that we distinguish between those things which are beyond doubt God's revelation and to which we must together adhere, and those other things on which, though we may need to adopt a policy, we cannot make a difference of opinion a matter of priority. For instance, you either do or do not have regional bishops in your church, but the Bible does not give us a clear direction. It is also hard to find a practical system that is open about the question of infant baptism and the nature of the ministry. We have to decide even while we acknowledge that other views are possible. But, within limits, these are questions altogether secondary to the revealed truths plainly taught in the Bible. If they were vital they would have been taught plainly.

The doctrinal basis of a Christian mind

We find ourselves, then, in this very strong situation. As Christians we believe with the New Testament writers that God has spoken. As we have seen from Hebrews 1:1–4, He spoke in time past in the Old Testament, but now in these last days supremely and finally in his Son. He also speaks (as Heb. 2 goes on to say) in the word that "was declared at first by the Lord, and it was attested to us by those who heard Him." Not forgetting that the Word of God is supremely Jesus himself, the New Testament also speaks of the gospel as "the word of God" (1 Thess. 2:13) and of the whole Christian revelation in the same phrase (1 Peter 1:22–25)—God has spoken. We have a word from God which has a content that we can spell out. Our duty, then, is to try to understand and apply it aright. We are not just thinking up and comparing opinions and systems. We are concerned to say and obey God's truth that he has so graciously given us. Like the scientist who has only some of the facts, we may have to say that we cannot see the whole, but we can nevertheless be certain of many aspects which we do see.

Unless we hold this conviction, we cannot really talk about having a Christian mind in any very meaningful sense. I have argued that a Christian mind arises out of revealed doctrine. The mind has to be remolded to operate from the *truths* that God has given us. Although they do not provide a complete system, and although on the other hand they can all be summarized as "in Christ," they do also provide an outline of truths that relate to each other and so form an incomplete (and to the professional philosopher a very unphilosophical) system or pattern of health-giving teachings.

4

A Christian mind
in philosophy

If the Bible does not give us a complete system of either ethics or
doctrine, it seems exceedingly improbable that we shall be able
to construct with any confidence a complete Christian philosophy or "world-and-life view." It may be possible to form an
outline. But a complete structure would involve some very
tentative shortcuts and guesswork. That might be a help to our
thinking in the field of philosophy and theoretical approaches to
life, but, even more than in the other two areas, I want to argue
that it also has serious dangers. Nevertheless, although we
should be very cautious about any attempts to construct a
complete Christian philosophy, I also want to argue that in the
Bible we have more than a totally piecemeal or ad hoc approach
to problems. We can, and indeed we must, approach problems
of life and thought, not only in terms of particular biblical
truths, but also in terms of broad principles and attitudes that
constitute a Christian outlook created by allowing God's revelation to mold our thinking and our priorities in life.

Sometimes the best response is an ad hoc appeal to a
particular truth or even to a particular verse that embodies it.
Our Lord himself responded to Satan's temptation in that way.
Three times he replied, "It is written," and he refused to allow
any argument (Matt. 4:1–11). David similarly was urged by his
companions in arms to kill King Saul when the opportunity

arose. He replied with a blunt "I will not put forth my hand against my lord; for his is the LORD's anointed" (1 Sam. 24:10). That was the end of the discussion! When the same kind of opportunity and the same pressure from his friends was repeated soon afterward, David replied in the same terms. He then, however, added that he believed in God's providence to remove Saul at the right time and in the right way (See 1 Sam. 26:10–11). There was an ad hoc response, but when further argument could not be avoided, it was backed up by the theological framework of his faith in God's ruling of the world. So with us today. There are times when the problems are simple problems of obedience and we must obey. If people (or the Devil) argue with us, we may have to go to the broader Christian perspective provided by our knowledge of God and his ways, but there is nothing to be ashamed of in an ad hoc response, and it may provide sufficient guidance and save a lot of qualifying discussion and possible compromise. Our Lord's example is surely an encouragement here. If we are tempted to steal it should be sufficient to say to ourselves, "Thou shalt not steal." A too sophisticated approach sometimes misses the sharp end of the biblical commands.

A New Testament example

If, as I have shown, Paul deals with the question of Christians going to law with one another in only seven verses in 1 Corinthians 6 by twice saying, "Do you not know. . . ?" and quoting the teaching of Christ, he does not deal with many problems so briefly or so directly. Even in this case his answer is not a proof text approach but the quotation of a basic truth. 1 Corinthians 1–4 is probably the best example in the New Testament of a thorough treatment of one particular issue. Paul starts with the problem of rivalries between parties in the Corinthian church (1 Cor. 1:10–12). He ends the discussion by bringing to bear on it a Christian view of the role of ministers and church planters like himself and Apollos, whose names were being used as party labels. One might think that that would have been enough to deal with it. First Corinthians 3:5–7, near the end of the discussion, reads as follows:

> What then is Apollos? What is Paul? Servants through whom you believed, as the Lord assigned to each. I planted, Apollos watered, but God gave the growth. So neither he who plants not he who waters is anything, but only God who gives the growth.

Could not Paul have said this at the beginning and cut out all that goes in between? In fact, he has gone to very considerable trouble to lay a far broader foundation for the solution to the problem. He has detected in this conflict of parties a fundamentally wrong attitude to human ability and wisdom. The Corinthians have too high a view of mere men and too low a view of the revelation of God. Therefore, before he answers their problems about ministers in terms of a Christian view of the ministry, he tackles the far broader question of revelation and the place of human wisdom in relation to the gospel. He lays a foundation that will help not only in this particular problem but in many others, one that is needed as part of the whole Christian outlook on culture, learning, theological scholarship, and Christian apologetics and evangelism. It is a basic part of a truly Christian outlook. What he writes could be summarized as follows:

a. The gospel of Christ crucified is essentially contrary to what men would, by the light of unaided reason and instinct, expect or wish to believe. Men think it stupid ("The word of the cross is folly to those who are perishing"). In reality, however, it is the power of God ("But to us who are being saved it is the power of God," 1 Cor. 1:18). God is bringing the cleverness of men to nothing (v. 19).

b. God chose to reveal the truth by a method and in a form that is deflating to human pride and contrary to what men expect from their own reasoning. This shows that it is in fact man who is stupid ("Has not God made foolish the wisdom of the world?" v. 20). For God has deliberately ordained things in such a way that man cannot reach a knowledge of God by mere human thinking, even when all the best of human wisdom is employed ("For since, in the wisdom of God, the world did not know God through wisdom," v. 21).

c. Even the Jews in their intense religiosity look in the wrong place for proof of what is true. The Greeks, equally, in their superb development of philosophy look only for truth that is the apex of human intelligence (v. 22).

d. We, however, preach a gospel that is offensive to both outlooks but is seen, by all who are called by God, to be the power and wisdom of God (vv. 23–24).

e. That makes us realize that God at his weakest is both stronger and wiser than men (v. 25). God in fact deliberately chose what is foolish in the world to shame the wise so that men could not boast before God that they had got the truth by their own moral or intellectual efforts (vv. 26–31). On the contrary, Jesus Christ is God's answer to the fact that man is intellectually and morally in the dark. Where man is helpless, Christ brings light and power (v. 30: "Christ Jesus, whom God made our wisdom, our righteousness and sanctification and redemption"). The Christian can boast only of what God has given—not of his abilities, gifts, understanding, righteousness, or advanced holiness of character. "Let him who boasts, boast of the Lord" (v. 31).

f. Not only the message itself, therefore, but also the method of presenting it has to be preserved from giving any impression that it is just another, but better, human philosophy, or that it is dependent on the superior abilities of the preacher. The cross cannot be made attractive by such human embellishments (2:1–5); they would distort and obscure the reality. This, however, is not to say that the Christian message is less than true wisdom (2:6–16). It is in fact God's truth (i.e., true wisdom), and Christians have been given the real insight into life. The Holy Spirit enables us to see what life is in fact like—how God sees it. Indeed, "we have the mind of Christ" (v. 16), even though that seems ridiculous to most people. Therefore human wisdom is not to be dealt with by better human wisdom but by divine revelation, lest anyone should glory in men (3:21) and fail to glory in the Lord (1:31).

g. Only after this long argument does Paul turn in chapter 4 to address directly the problem that had been raised and to show that ministers are only stewards of God's revelation (the message is not the product of human intellect) and his *servants* (they are not bosses of the church).

The point of this example is not that Paul is using a steam hammer to crack a nut, but that he is tackling a particular problem by reemphasizing wider aspects of truth. In so doing he shows us that practical questions can be adequately dealt with only by a wide-ranging Christian outlook. By his method he was encouraging the Christians at Corinth to solve practical problems by thinking how these things look in the light of Christian doctrine on a wide scale. His *method* is what I want to stress. He has discovered in this problem an area where a Christian outlook differs fundamentally from that of even the most able non-Christian thinking, and so he deals with it in a radical—and he hopes final—way. In doing that he shows us what the mind of Christ is like in one of its basic aspects. His approach is far from being ad hoc or piecemeal. It is truly theological, going back to God and his revelation.

A Christian "onlook"

This is one of the passages that leads us to describe the Christian mind as a whole *outlook* controlled by revealed truth and at the same time to deny that it is either a philosophy or a systematic world view. Indeed, if there were such a word in English it might be better to talk of a Christian "onlook" or even "inlook." The Christian is not just looking out of one corner of reality to view the rest. He has a new vantage point from which he can see the whole of life better than anyone else. In fact this very passage emphasized that we must not *reduce* the gospel to such a small thing as a philosophical system. If we did that we would have substituted a merely human outlook for God's revealed "onlook," and God's wisdom includes the fact, as Paul states in 1 Corinthians 1, that man's wisdom is never able to grasp the whole picture or to get to the heart of reality. A philosophical system must answer the questions that philosophers ask. The

Christian revelation is set out in terms of the questions that God asks—questions regarding such matters as sin and grace; questions that are far more fundamental, but are avoided by philosophy. When people try to make Christianity into a philosophy, they force it into a mold which it cannot fit, because its essence is not philosophical but theological. Paul does not hesitate to call those "fools" who think that a clever philosophy is the answer to life. Man always misses the point; and the more impressive his systems are, the more they are a hindrance to the discovery of fundamental truth, because people think that they have already arrived.

A Christian philosophy, if one were constructed, would on this view not be recognizable as a philosophy, because it would start with God and his revelation. It would not be unfairly dismissed in the philosophical schools as "theology." There must always be Christians whose job it is to grapple with philosophical thinking, and there could be philosophical systems that are *not inconsistent* with Christian revelation. But they will be merely philosophies, unable to answer the most important questions, dealing only with questions raised by mere men. As an exercise in apologetics—answering men's questions and criticism of Christianity—philosophy is important, but not fundamental. What is more, like Christian political parties, philosophies will never be 100 percent Christian. We are not given a blueprint for such detailed areas of thought, and much of the resulting system is, biblically speaking, guesswork.

Some dangers of intellectual system-builders

The biblical view of a Christian mind is therefore, I would argue, something different from what many of those who ask for a consistent Christian mind are wanting. They speak as if they expected to be able to construct a more or less complete and watertight intellectual system. From this they could be expected to read off Christian answers to every philosophical issue and to every problem without too much difficulty. Indeed they sometimes say that without such a Christian philosophy we are bound to make many mistakes, to be inconsistent in many ways and so to fail to bring glory to God as we should. Others insist that we need to develop cultural analysis or the sociology of ideas and ideologies so as to beat the non-Christian intellectuals at their own game. I do not find that kind of emphasis on the importance of intellectual analysis in the New Testament. There is a place for it, but I believe that those who think it is the answer will be sadly disappointed because they have lost sight of the biblical agenda, as I will argue further below.

To take one example, many of those influenced by the "Amsterdam Philosophy" of Dooyeweerd and Vollenhoven (see Appendix) say that until we have developed a proper Christian philosophy of education, we can do very little as Christian educators. We shall thus be guilty of grave inconsistencies, and possibly do as much damage as we do good, by being involved in education. To this I would say that the facts are against that claim. Indeed in some ways it is evident nonsense. First, although they have talked like this for more than fifty years, those concerned still cannot produce the Christian philosophy of education that they hope for. They have produced some helpful and constructive criticism of what other educators do, but they still cannot produce a worked-out philosophy of education that can claim to be consistently Christian and can be applied to the practical tasks of teaching. Meanwhile nearly two generations of teachers have come and gone and have in fact often done very good work as Christian educators. They did not give up in despair for lack of a Christian philosophy of what they were doing, but they followed the biblical method of applying revealed truth to their professional work as they went along. There are good Christian schools, and good Christian staff in other schools, whose work is impressive and fruitful, even where they would not come near to satisfying these more theoretical thinkers. They are often nearer to what the Bible means by a Christian mind than are those who try to build a Christian philosophy of education.

Further, if a complete theological or ethical system involves shortcuts, distortions, and areas of uncertainty, a complete Christian philosophy would do so even more. It would save us from some mistakes, but it would create some others, and they would be all the more serious because what is propounded would be thought to be authoritatively Christian. This has in fact happened. Christian educational institutions based on such thinking are not in every way a model, and the damage is serious because pupils and parents are led to believe that all that goes on is Christian. Like the mapmakers who fill in the valleys when they can have firm evidence only of the mountaintops, they are certain often to get it wrong, however skillfully the work is done. The world is not as regular and unchangeable as we would like it to be. This would not matter so much if we did not then ask people to be guided by our map, as if it were all the result of careful observation and were providing a reliable guide. We ought really to leave huge areas blank, or if we fill them in, to fill them in in a way that makes it plain that these parts are guesswork.

Meanwhile we can also be easily distracted from the more important task of applying biblical truth that is clear to the varied tasks before us. This has happened on a large scale. People have begun to think of Christian philosophy rather than the Bible as having the answer to life. While people choose a Christian philosophy, the varied and changing issues before the church have to be tackled by others who are less philosophically inclined but more practical and sometimes closer to the Bible. An acute observer of European "Christian philosophies" remarked to me that their greatest weakness is in their practical outworking. Here the fruits of such thinking are very meager. Often the practical policies to which they lead are either trite or very controversial. They have their place in the analysis and criticism of other philosophies, but they do not easily relate to practical realities in the way that Bible truth does. For instance, the idea that the children of Christian parents should be withdrawn into Christian schools, universities, or trade associations, is one such controversial fruit of some kinds of Christian philosophy, not of the teaching of the Bible, which does not even hint at such a thing.

A world-and-life view?

There are others who are more modest in their aims. They agree that a complete system is not possible or, if possible, has many hidden dangers in it. Nevertheless, they talk convincingly of the need to develop a sufficiently consistent world-and-life view for us to have clear guidelines in relation to both secular thought and practical action. The term *world-and-life view* is in fact quite ambiguous. To some it means much the same thing as a Christian philosophy and is thought of in extremely abstract philosophical terms. What I have said above applies, I believe, with equal force to those who are really calling a Christian philosophy by a less formidable name. It is useful in the service of apologetics and in discovering faults in the secular thinking that so easily influence us unawares. The important faults are, however, in fact theological—wrong views of God and man, etc. Our defense is biblical and not philosophical thinking.

Other writers have something far more modest in mind and mean only a rather systematic Christian outlook. So long as the framework of this is explicitly biblical teaching, then it is what I believe the Bible would mean by a Christian mind for those with intellectual gifts. I see Francis Schaeffer as fitting into this last category. He has never claimed nor wanted a complete intellectual system as some others do.

Even here there are dangers, though they are not insurmountable. A world view easily changes the agenda of the church. The New Testament not only gives us our methods, but also surely gives us the *agenda for God's people*. The New Testament Epistles focus the attention of the whole church—educated and uneducated—on the great themes of the gospel that God has revealed together with the outworking of those truths in practical life. The New Testament writers constantly stress that God saved us so that "we should be holy and blameless before him . . . to the praise of his glorious grace" (Eph. 1:4–6; and see Titus 2:14). To that end we are directed to give attention first of all to our estimate of ourselves as God's people, and then to personal morality, home life, church life, work life, and life as citizens of the state. We must put these things, which the Bible puts first, as first on our agenda. If a world-and-life view will help us do that, it will be a great blessing. If it leads us to think that we can push these things aside for more intellectual tasks, it will mislead the church most seriously. In any case, what may be appropriate for the more philosophically minded Christian is often inappropriate for others. Any suggestion that a Christian world-and-life view is somehow superior to the constant application of biblical truths to each day and each issue as it comes along is a dangerous conceit.

We need Christian thinkers who can systematize biblical truth and relate it to our culture and its outlook, exposing what is false and confirming what is true in it. Those who are working out a Christian world-and-life view in such terms are doing a very useful job. From a New Testament perspective, however, it is not more but less important than a right attitude toward your parents, children, marriage partner, job, and church. It is these practical concerns that are to come at the top of our agenda. Many who are advocating a Christian world-and-life view in this moderate sense would wholeheartedly agree with that. They are simply trying to use their intellectual gifts in the service of the church so that we may add to a solid personal morality, in obedience to the plain commands of the Bible, a sharper critique of our times, and a more consistent constructive Christian framework of thought. Francis and Edith Schaeffer, for instance, not only do the latter, but equally have written penetratingly about the nature of Christian love in practice and the enrichment of the Christian home. Those who have fastened solidly on the intellectual aspects of Christian world views have often been disappointed at the meager fruits of such a purely intellectual structure because they have overthrown the biblical priorities and forgotten the biblical agenda.

It is understandable that writers like Blamires in the Catholic tradition (he is a high-church Anglican) would argue for a complete Christian world-and-life view. In that tradition there should be a complete moral casuistry—a system of rules and detailed conclusions from which one can read off the right moral response in almost every situation. Those who think in this way also look for a more or less complete and authoritative theological system, which is not secondary to Scripture but has the authoritative status of church or papal teaching. It would not be inconsistent for them to ask for a complete Christian philosophy, sociology, psychology, etc., to match. In the Reformation tradition, however, a complete Christian philosophy is very difficult to justify. Those in the Reformation tradition do not believe in a complete casuistic system in ethics, nor do they believe in a complete theological system. In theology the Calvinist and Lutheran traditions have come nearer to a complete doctrinal system than have other Protestant traditions, but the systematic theologies and the great Reformation and post-Reformation Confessions in those traditions (such as the Westminster Confession) are always seen as secondary to Scripture and confess some areas of uncertainty or leave some issues on one side. When they do come down decisively on questions which in practice divide Bible-believing Christians (such as pacifism, infant baptism, the communion service, and church order, limited atonement, and whether there are one, two, or three covenants), then usually they should profess a greater humility about their conclusions than they do. Nevertheless one can understand those people who believe you can have a complete and authoritative theological system, if they think you can *also* have both a complete system of ethical casuistry and a complete world-and-life view. It is probably significant that the thinkers in the Dooyeweerdian school have often commented that their Christian philosophy is better appreciated by many Roman Catholics than by most Protestants. The reason, I believe, is that the Roman Catholic thinkers accept the concept of a complete and totally self-consistent system of thought, whereas for good reasons, as we have discussed, most Protestants do not and should not.

It is in accord with this approach that Joshua, when charged with leadership of God's people for a huge military and social campaign, was given one great assurance: "I will be with you; I will not fail you or forsake you." Then he was given the one essential tool: "This book of the law shall not depart out of your mouth, but you shall meditate on it day and night, that you may be careful to do according to all that is written in it; for then you shall make your way prosperous, and then you shall have good success" (Josh. 1:8). It was not a simple rule-book—he had to *meditate* on it day and night; but he needed no other intellectual tool. We are brought back to the *sufficiency* of the Scripture. It deals with the really fundamental issues of life. Neither philosophy, nor sociology, nor psychology, nor any other of the useful human disciplines do that. They all deal with side issues by comparison. What we need to be able to do—and it is the one thing essential for the Christian life and warfare—is to be able to see how biblical truth bears on life. That is not something obvious. We have to think and meditate upon it and seek the Holy Spirit's enlightenment.

The point is well illustrated by what happens when Christians try to develop a "Christian political position." Whenever this has been attempted the results have proved disappointing because, however much people try to disown all non-Christian elements, they end up with a political ideology that is, first, not accepted by many other true Christians (is it the Democrats or the Republicans, the Moral Majority, or a form of socialistic pacifism?) Second, it is quickly out of date in its priorities. Third, it contains elements that are very hard to justify as specifically Christian. Its guesswork is never altogether convincing and it is sometimes a real embarrassment to other Christians. Finally, a Christian philosophy and a Christian political party raise expectations that they cannot fulfill and so bring disillusionment both to the Christian and to those camp followers who are impressed by their promises.

This is not to deny the usefulness of Christian thinking in the area of philosophy or politics. Indeed Christian philosophizing for some people is a must, because their world overlaps with the world of philosophic thought. We have, for instance, to take sides in the discussion about idealism or realism, and we will almost certainly conclude that some kind of realism is *most constant with* a Christian view of the world as created by God. Not all the questions asked by philosophers, however, are important for most Christians. Nevertheless, that does not mean that Christians with the right gifts should not spend their energies in this area. Indeed, we need Christians in philosophy as we need Christian thinkers in politics, medicine, psychology, education, law, and every other discipline. It does not follow that they should develop a complete philosophy, any more than it follows that every parent must have a complete "philosophy" of Christian parenthood. They need an outline of relevant biblical truths and they need to help one another see how these apply to their particular world. The right way of developing a Christian mind is to think in accordance with revealed truth. That means that the teaching of the Bible is the fundamental area in which we need both knowledge and understanding. Sometimes we must be willing to say plainly, like Paul, that the world's wise men are "fools" because, in all their wisdom, they have missed the whole point of life. When we do that we must expect them in turn to think that we are fools because we have not answered all their questions, and yet we believe we do have the key to life.

The biblical pattern

We do not have a *complete* world-and-life view or philosophy given to us. We have something far better and far more practical. It is for the ordinary Christian a network of revealed truth that enables him to bring to bear on every situation those principles that ought to be kept in mind. It should not worry us if we do not have ready answers to the world's agenda of questions. They ask these questions partly because they have lost the key to knowledge and wisdom. When we discuss them we shall often have to say that the questions are wrongly conceived and the whole of life needs to be looked at in another, theological way; that is to say, in the light of God and his truth.

Jesus set us this example in refusing to answer some of the hard questions put to him. When the Sadducees came with a story about a woman who had been widowed seven times, having been married to seven brothers in turn, and asked, "In the resurrection whose wife will she be?" Jesus replied by saying, "You are wrong . . . you know neither the scriptures nor the power of God." "When they rise from the dead, they neither marry nor are given in marriage" (see Mark 12:23–27). When he asked a trick question, "Is it lawful to pay taxes to Caesar?" he did not answer their question. He replied with a principle so profound that in each generation since, Christians have found it a mine of practical guidance. "Render to Caesar the things that are Caesar's, and to God the things that are God's" (Mark 12:17). Some questions Jesus simply refused to answer at all. We must not be ashamed to admit that there are not clear Christian answers to some philosophical and other problems, because they are the wrong questions.

A complete and correct world-and-life view would correspond to a God's-eye view, and no one should ever pretend that we possess that. God has given us, in human terms, some parts of his view of life, but he has not set them in a complete system—probably because man could not possibly grasp it correctly if he did.

Yet Christians do have the "light of life." As Peter puts it, we have in Scripture "a lamp shining in a dark place." The Bible is a *sufficient* guide "that the man of God may be complete." It does not provide a neat and complete intellectual system. It provides a framework of truth that stands for all time and gives us all we actually need. We are to learn to apply that to all the varied and changing situations we face, and that challenges us with an ongoing task that is always a living application of God's Word and Spirit to our own life and thought.

Our wisdom which in the face of the world's wisdom is the wisdom which is expressed in Christ, who is "made our wisdom, our righteousness and sanctification and redemption," and it is to this theme of wisdom that we must now turn.

5

Wisdom, intellectualism, and anti-intellectualism

We can approach this whole subject of the Christian mind from another angle by exploring the biblical theme of wisdom. While the Christian community has sometimes been divided by arguments for and against an intellectual Christianity, the Bible seems to bypass that question by urging us to seek and to hold onto wisdom. In the Old Testament this is said to start with the "fear of the Lord." Psalm 111:10 and Proverbs 9:10 both tell us that "the fear of the LORD is the beginning of knowledge." In the New Testament, it is Christ himself who is "our wisdom" (1 Cor. 1:30; see also Col. 2:3). Indeed, we could say that the New Testament equivalent of "the fear of the LORD" in the Old Testament is personal faith in Christ. Without that personal faith we have not begun to see what life is really all about, just as, in Old Testament times, without this personal trust and awe for the living God who had revealed himself as the LORD,[1] people's understanding of life simply had not got the right center. These two concepts are very close to each other.

The problem is to know what these claims imply. If the fear of the Lord is the beginning of wisdom and knowledge, and if the

---

[1] The word translated LORD (using small capitals) is always Yahweh or Jehovah in Hebrew, and the Greek equivalent is often applied to Jesus in the New Testament quotations from the Old, e.g., 1 Corinthians 1:31; 2:16.

men without Christ are fools just when they are professing to be wise (Rom. 1:22), does it mean that all human knowledge is really false when personal faith is lacking? Is the non-Christian totally in the dark? Does it mean also that all human wisdom without Christ has to be seen not only as foolish, but also as an enemy of the truth, as some have concluded?

Anti-intellectualism

Starting with passages such as 1 Corinthians 1:18, 20—"The word of the cross is folly to those who are perishing, but to us who are being saved it is the power of God. . . . Has not God made foolish the wisdom of the world?"—it has been argued that the whole intellectual endeavor of men is futile and that Christians should not waste their time on it or risk being infected with its folly. The right policy, according to this view, is to "keep the simple gospel" and leave the world to do its own philosophizing and speculation. We argued in chapter 1 that this view is defective from the point of view of our Lord's emphasis on the need to love God with all our minds, and that, apart from that command, Christians are in practice forced to move into Christian thinking beyond the simple gospel if they are to try to please God in daily life. I now want to show that a more careful examination of what the Bible does in fact say about wisdom will make us value and not decry Christian thinking, though it may not make us want to be all intellectual. This discussion will also make us recognize that non-Christian thinking may not be totally at fault, and that we can learn important things from non-Christian thinkers even when we reject their overall perspective on life and their own priorities.

In one absolutely fundamental respect the "simple gospel" school, which has often been called "pietist," must have our profound admiration. The Pietists often kept to truly Christian priorities when nearly everyone else has been drifting further and further into a merely humanistic (or political) outlook in the place of biblical truth. They have been the backbone of missionary and evangelistic endeavor. They have preserved a rich personal and corporate devotional life. They have been strong in personal ethics and Christian fellowship. There have been times when the Pietists have been almost the only people keeping to these things. We thank God for those who in this way preserved the gospel witness in dark periods of the church's history and spread the gospel to new lands at great self-sacrifice. For all the modern criticism of the cultural insensitiveness and other shortcomings of the early missions of Africa, Asia, and Latin American, the fact is that, without them, there would not now be a large and flourishing Christian church at all. They planted the churches and built them up, and a very large percentage of them were in the pietist tradition. Without their narrow emphasis on personal salvation they and the churches they founded would not likely still be healthy.

This noble tradition has nevertheless not taken sufficiently seriously what passages like 1 Corinthians 1–3 actually say. When Paul had finished emphasizing the futility of human wisdom for bringing us to God (1 Cor. 1:21, "in the wisdom of God, the world did not know God through wisdom"), he went on to speak of "Christ Jesus, whom God made our *wisdom*, our righteousness and sanctification and redemption" (1:30). Then, he says in the next chapter:

> Yet among the mature we do impart *wisdom*, although it is not a wisdom of this age or of the rulers of this age, who are doomed to pass away. But we impart a secret and hidden *wisdom of God*. . . .The spiritual man judges all things, but is himself to be judged by no one. "For who has known the mind of the Lord so as to instruct him?" But we have the mind of Christ (2:6–7, 15–16).

The Christian, then, has true wisdom, is able to see all things in their true perspective (judges *all* things). He sees life in a truly Christian way; that is to say he sees things as they really are. He has "the mind of Christ." The trouble with the world's wisdom is that it is only half-wisdom—and in making the half into the whole it ends up by being grossly misleading. As Paul himself puts it in another passage to the same church (2 Cor. 10:5), "We destroy arguments and every proud obstacle to the knowledge of God, and take every thought captive to obey Christ." In biblical terms, therefore, the "simple gospel" pietism does not go far enough. It is the right foundation: but the New Testament sees Christians as building on that foundation to bring *all* thinking and *all* action into captivity to Christ. We cannot allow large areas of our life to be uncontrolled by what God has said to us about it: and if we do, we shall probably fall into the hair-raising errors of life and thought that had arisen in the Corinthian church and can still arise in Christian circles today. *Every* thought must be brought captive to Christ if we are to be full-grown and mature Christians. As Paul puts it in 1 Corinthians 14:20, "Brethren, do not be children in your thinking; be babes in evil, but in thinking [literally minds] be mature," or as the Authorized Version has it, "in understanding be men." An anti-intellectualism that allows us to run away from the challenge of thinking Christianly cannot therefore be the right answer. It has frequently led to the loss by the church of many of its able members. They cannot honestly avoid the questions they face. They are not being unspiritual in trying to grapple with them, but have to go elsewhere if they are met only with suspicion by their fellow believers. They therefore easily look for help from non-Christian intellectuals and suffer accordingly.

Intellectualism

Faced with an anti-intellectual tradition Christians have easily overreacted into forms of intellectualism that are even more dangerous in the other direction. Because of their frustration at the refusal of an older generation to do some necessary Christian thinking, it has not been uncommon for Christians to put their confidence in mental activity and to delight in being labeled "intellectual." What has happened all too often is that they begin to believe that the problems of life and of the church can be solved merely by thinking. Those who go this way, of course, are usually the more academically gifted Christians who are in any case in danger of intellectual pride. (Others are more tempted to other forms of pride. We each think that our own gifts are the really important ones that the church needs!) Especially when a new generation is better educated than the last, it is not surprising if the real wisdom of the older generation is thought of as too simplistic, and what is put in its place is too self-confident about human reason and knowledge of the world. Admittedly each generation and each culture needs to think things out for itself. We cannot have a Christian mind handed to us on a plate by elders, foreign missionaries, or great Christians of the past. Whatever profound Christian understanding they may have had has to be worked through for ourselves in terms of our own world, whether it is less or more sophisticated that theirs. But merely thinking will not solve the problem, and relying on our ability to think for ourselves will prove a snare. Thinking is called for in a Christian, but it must be a humble sitting under the revelation of God. It is not even "Christian philosophy," as I pointed out in the last chapter.

It is related of Professor A. Schlatter (a German evangelical theologian) that an overseas research student, when introduced to him, stepped forward to shake hands and said, "I am delighted to meet you, Professor Schlatter. I hear that you are one of the few theologians left in Europe who takes his stand firmly on the Bible." Professor Schlatter looked the man up and down for a moment and then replied, "On the contrary! I sit under the Bible."

Intellectual activity that does not sit under the Bible, but makes any form of human knowledge (even a theological dogma) its primary data, has become a form of humanism. The more thoughtful Christians, trying to grapple with the world's thought-systems, can easily be overwhelmed and lose a distinctively Christian position—substituting another mere thought-system for the world's. This happens most easily when they lack the support and encouragement of the church to go on and capture fresh intellectual ground for Christ. Sometimes they meet only suspicion and criticism from their less academic fellow Christians. The situation is not helped at all by running away from intellectual activity. The answer is seriously to try to bring every thought "captive to obey Christ." This is part of fighting the good fight of faith, and we must help one another to do it well. Failure to do so will result in some Christians opting out and drifting into a reliance on scholarship or their own intellectual ability. "Claiming to be wise, they become fools" is Paul's epitaph on the secular thinking of his day, and, sadly, this could be written over much self-consciously intellectual Christianity down the ages.

The definition of wisdom

In contrast with both the anti-intellectual and the intellectual responses, the Bible tells us to seek wisdom. Wisdom in the Bible is a very practical thing. It is spoken of very much as we have spoken of a Christian mind. It can be defined as *the ability to see the true nature of things and how, in the light of that, we should live*. In the Book of Proverbs, for instance, it has three main strands: knowledge, understanding, and practical know-how (in the light of the knowledge and understanding). Words like understanding, insight, and prudence rub shoulders in its definitions with knowledge and instruction on the one hand and with wise dealing, righteousness, and justice on the other. Understanding depends on knowledge, but has to lead in turn to wise action. For instance, Proverbs 1:2–7, which sets out the aim of that book, reads as follows:

> That men may know wisdom and instruction, understand words of *insight*, receive instruction in *wise dealing, righteousness, justice,* and *equity*; that *prudence* may be given to the simple, *knowledge* and *discretion* to the youth—the wise man also may hear and increase in *learning*, and the man of *understanding* acquire *skill*, to understand a proverb and a figure, the words of the wise and their riddles. The fear of the LORD is the beginning of knowledge; fools despise wisdom and instruction.

Similarly, Solomon was specially promised by God that he would be given wisdom, and he is consistently spoken of as supremely endowed with it. His wisdom typifies the biblical ideal, and he showed that wisdom at the start of his reign in his famous judgment of the two prostitutes (1 Kings 3). These two women shared a house. Each claimed to be the mother of a living child and not the mother of another child, which had died. Solomon's wisdom in this case consisted first of understanding a fundamental aspect of true motherhood and then of seeking out a way to discover who was the actual mother of the living child. Confronted by these not altogether reliable witnesses, he asked for a sword to be brought and he offered, rather dramatically, to cut the living child in two and give each mother half. One woman said, "No, I would rather that she had the child alive. Don't kill it." The other said, "It shall be neither mine nor yours; divide it." Solomon then answered, "Give the living child to the first woman, and by no means slay it; she is its mother." It is recorded that "All Israel . . . stood in awe of the king, because they perceived that the wisdom of God was in him, to render justice." His wisdom consisted in "understanding," leading to practical justice. The Book of Proverbs illustrates further what kind of thing wisdom is seen to be. Thus wisdom is that kind of understanding of the real state of affairs (which includes moral knowledge) that enables us to act rightly, and in the case of a king to judge justly. It depends absolutely on real understanding, but it is practical rather that academic.

True wisdom and human knowledge

In the Book of Proverbs, however, we discover what is at first sight a surprising thing. Although the fear of the Lord is the beginning of both knowledge and wisdom, Proverbs includes many sayings collected from unbelievers. Chapter 30, for instance, records the sayings of Agur, who seems specifically to deny that he has the "knowledge of the Holy One." A fair number of the proverbs, indeed, appear to have been collected from other sources and certainly they are very closely paralleled in the writings of some Egyptians and other people who were not believers at all in the Old Testament sense. Even Solomon's judgment discussed above was not in itself something that could not have been carried out by an unbeliever. Much of the Book of Proverbs seems to be common sense based on a scale of values that would be shared by many, but not all, unbelievers. Take, for example, the following: "Pride goes before destruction, and a haughty spirit before a fall" (16:18); "A hot-tempered man stirs up strife, but he who is slow to anger quiets contention" (15:18); "The way of a fool is right in his own eyes, but a wise man listens to advice" (12:15); "Do not boast about tomorrow, for you do not know what a day may bring forth" (27:1); "A man who flatters his neighbor spreads a net for his feet" (29:5); "Wine is a mocker, strong drink a brawler; and whoever is led astray by it is not wise" (20:1).

The writer even urges us to learn from the ant: "Go to the ant, O sluggard; consider her ways, and be wise. Without having any chief, officer or ruler, she prepares her food in summer, and gathers her sustenance in harvest" (6:6).

Further, the understanding that unbelievers have can be at least relatively wise. Daniel and his friends were among the wise men of Babylon, and even though they were ten times better than the others, it was still seen as a relative matter (Dan. 1:20; cf. 5:11–12). Babylon had "wisdom and knowledge" that were so successful that they led the nation astray into pride and self-confidence (Isa. 47:10). The prince of Tyre is said to have been "wiser than Daniel," but he was proud and considered himself "as wise as a god," therefore he was judged (Ezek. 28:1–10).

Similarly, in the New Testament, the wisdom of unbelievers is still called "wisdom." Jesus thanks the Father that the truth of the gospel "is hidden from the *wise* and prudent." He even speaks of "the sons of this world as being more shrewd in their own generation than the sons of light," that is, wiser within their own perspective and for their own purposes. The Bible does not dismiss all human knowledge and understanding as nonsense. It consistently points out its fundamental inadequacy for the knowledge of God and of his will, but it does not despise its practical usefulness or those of its insights that are true. See, for example, Titus 1:12–13, where Paul quotes a pagan poet and comments, "This testimony is true." Note that this is not an evangelistic address but is instruction to a fellow Christian.

Is wisdom then relative?

The Christian, therefore, does not have a monopoly on wisdom. If there are wise men of the world who are in fact fools, there are also some very foolish Christians, and we have all met them. They have never got beyond the very beginning of wisdom. The Christian who has the right perspective (the fear of the Lord) can still be a fool in many areas. If that were not so, most of Proverbs (which was written to help people live wisely) would not have been necessary. Having the fundamental attitude right does not mean that one automatically has all the answers, any more than having love gives us automatic ethical guidelines, or having faith in Christ solves all doctrinal questions. We still need to learn and to obey true wisdom both in principle *and* in practical detail. Our human natures are too prone to guide us into folly, such as giving priority to whatever offers short-term advantage. Christians have often made the great mistake of thinking that, because the fear of the Lord is the *beginning* of wisdom, it is also the *whole of wisdom*. It is not so, and the Bible is there to show us both what wisdom is in principle, and also how to develop wisdom for every task (i.e., to be renewed in mind). Christians are always subject to the temptation of thinking that, merely because they are Christians, they have nothing to learn about how to build up their marriage or how to run a Christian organization, for instance. A good non-Christian marriage counselor or doctor or accountant may be able to help us greatly. Experts in military strategy may have useful principles for strategy in other areas.[2]

The failure to recognize the need for the Christian to *grow in wisdom* is a source of many tragedies in the church. A Christian can too easily be self-confident and not pay attention to common sense or to relevant wisdom about health, personal relationships, educational or administrative experience. Many Christian marriages have come to grief because they felt it unspiritual to ask advice when strains developed. Some of the wisdom is in the Book of Proverbs, but by no means all. Compared with Christians, who may want to live as if they were all angels, the world is sometimes wiser about the dangers of

---

[2] For example, Admiral Mahan's dictum, which used to be displayed at the Dartmouth Naval College and has often been discussed in Christian organizations: "When you are trying to accomplish something, you should first decide what is the final object you are seeking to attain and then never lose sight of it."

exposing ourselves to temptation (in handling money, for example), because it is realistic in its assessment of human weaknesses.

The non-Christian, then, does have useful knowledge and often useful understanding. He may also see how to work out that understanding in practice.

Career counseling, for instance, may be very helpful to a Christian. The problem comes when the advice is based on a purely humanistic scale of values, but allowance can be made for that. If, for example, you are advised to follow a particular profession, first because "I think you would enjoy the work and do well at it," and second because "It offers big rewards financially," as a Christian you will have to try to avoid being tempted by the second but will not ignore the relevance of the first. The Christian will have other criteria that a non-Christian counselor will miss—for instance, what gifts is God giving him for *service* to men? But he must accept that the counselor may have unique knowledge as well as accumulated experience which should not be ignored and which deserve, in their limited area of application, the title of wisdom.

Christian and non-Christian wisdom

The difference between Christian and non-Christian wisdom is, therefore, not so much in terms of details but at the fundamental level. The whole perspective on life is different. That comes from personal faith and depends (as 1 Cor. 1–3 stresses), not on human cleverness, but on the fact that God has spoken and told us what human wisdom will never discover by itself. Where the non-Christian is most confident that he has the answers to life is where he is most foolish. Not only, as Pascal has it, is it true that "the heart has its reasons which reason knows nothing of," but the unregenerate heart and mind simply cannot reach up to a true understanding of life and therefore substitute one that is partly or wholly false. The greatest achievement of reason is to accept its own insufficiency and to allow men to ask God to speak. Proud autonomous man is the greatest fool at the fundamental level. And yet, partly because he has perhaps given all his energies to some limited area of human experience, he may be a very useful source of limited wisdom in that area. He may have good and useful knowledge and understanding even while he has missed the beginning of true knowledge and true wisdom. He does not know what life is all about, but he may understand some of its mechanisms better than anyone else. There are wise non-Christian doctors, teachers, farmers, etc. For many purposes we will seek out such a person even if in biblical terms he is a wise fool. This is for practical purposes better than a foolish wise man—a Christian who thinks that his faith makes him automatically more discerning in everything. Certain Christian political leaders seem to have failed for this reason. They were good men but lacked the necessary political wisdom. At another level of need the church should consult experts before making alterations to its buildings, whether those experts are Christian or not.

Wisdom thus starts with a true perspective on life, but even with a wrong perspective the non-Christian may be wise in many areas, while the Christian may never have used his right perspective to go beyond the elementary phases. The situation is like that of the professional in some field of knowledge faced with the experienced amateur. Scientific medicine, for instance, has to be very critical of native medicine and folklore, but sometimes that amateur medicine is right. Long before penicillin was discovered, some farmers in Britain used to keep moldy buns because, they said, when they were strapped onto a cut, it healed better. The reason evidently was that moldy buns grow a fine culture of *Penicillium!*

On the other hand, we should not devalue the contribution that professional wisdom can make. Experience of real life may enable the amateur to teach the professional what he might miss owing to a too theoretical approach, but he cannot replace the man who has the right *principles* for dealing with the subject.

Respect for knowledge and scholarship

The emphasis on wisdom in both the Old and New Testaments, therefore, gives us no encouragement to be either anti-intellectual (which is a cop-out and almost a form of cowardice) or intellectual (which is usually a form of overconfidence or pride in the ability of reason). The uneducated man who boasts of his lack of education and the scholar who politely lets you know how important his learning is are equally conceited and equally lack wisdom. The Bible leaves us with a duty to acquire all the useful knowledge and understanding that we can from any source. When the leaders of the rise of science in the seventeenth century, such as Francis Bacon, talked of two books, "The Book of God's Word" and "The Book of God's Works," they made a rather too neat division of life into two categories; but their point was valid in principle. God has given us the book of his Word to show us the fundamental nature of reality and to give us the guidance we need for thought and life. But he has also given us the ability to read nature and human experience to some extent and, according to our gifts, we have a duty to do both and to learn from those who are better informed than we are in both.

The Christian who improves himself intellectually should be doing so not because that in itself takes him nearer to biblical truth. It may equally well take him away from it. But he follows this track because he has the relevant gifts and sees the need to use them in the battle for the truth of God in these particular areas. He is in no way a better Christian; neither is he more fully loving God with his mind that is the Christian whose gifts are less academic. The gifts needed to be a good family man or a mother of young children or an office receptionist may not be so well paid, but they need every bit as much wisdom. Indeed, the concept of wisdom is a great leveler because we can all see that some very intellectual people lack both Christian wisdom and even basic human wisdom in their personal relationships. They may be highly successful academics, politicians, businessmen, military or trade union leaders, etc., from whom we can learn things in their own field. If, however, at the same time they have missed the whole point of life, or if in the very important questions of life, such as their relations with their marriage partner and children, colleagues and neighbors, they are very unskilled, then they lack true wisdom, and their intellectual expertise will not help them. We must be willing to respect and learn from scholarship, but we must acknowledge its limitations. As James 3:13, 17 has it: "Who is wise and understanding among you? By his good life let him show his works in the meekness of wisdom. . . . But the wisdom from above is first pure, then peaceable, gentle, open to reason, full of mercy and good fruits."

There is, however, no excuse for deliberate childishness. It is not humility, but rather immaturity, to talk and act in a way that is ridiculous for an adult. As 1 Corinthians 14:20 has it: "Do not be children in your thinking; be babes in evil, but in thinking be mature." Yet there is no superior Christian maturity for the intellectual. That was one of the mistakes of Gnosticism. As Colossians 1:28 expresses it, the apostle was "warning *every* man and teaching *every* man in *all* wisdom, that we may present every man mature in Christ." F. F. Bruce, in commenting on 1 Corinthians 1:28, expresses it thus: "There are no heights of Christian wisdom that are not within the reach of all, by the power of divine grace."

The biblical concept of wisdom means, then, that, when we try to develop a Christian mind, we respect and are thankful for human knowledge and learning from whatever source, while we are always on our guard lest some basically non-Christian presuppositions are being smuggled into the way it is presented. Even Moses, that great lawgiver and administrator of God's revelation, had to learn something about administration from his father-in-law, who was at best an entirely new convert to the faith (Exod. 18:10–12). When Jethro saw what was happening in the administration of justice, he told Moses that he must practice much more delegation of responsibility. Moses accepted this advice and acted on it (Exod. 18:13–27). So there is a place for listening to the unasked for advice of your father- or mother-in-law! The whole wealth of revealed wisdom that had been given to Moses had not saved him from a mistake in this area, and the experience of a shrewd and observant man coming in from outside Israel, and going away again soon after, was needed. Perhaps Jethro was the first ever business consultant.

It is said of Ahithophel that "the counsel which Ahithophel gave was as if one consulted the oracle of God" (2 Sam. 16:23).

This is to say, he was almost infallibly wise in his field. Both David and his rebellious son Absalom regarded him like that, and David's prayer that Ahithophel's counsel would be turned to foolishness was not answered in those terms at all. Having turned from David to support Absalom, he still gave the very best advice. But he was a mean and conceited traitor, who committed suicide as soon as his advice was not taken. Although his general outlook was foolishness in the extreme, his detailed advice in his field was marvelously wise.

A good modern example here is the discussion about the environment. The part played by Christian thinking in ecological discussions has been greatly distorted. Many disasters, such as the early dust bowls, were due to plain, but not culpable, ignorance of the possible consequences of policies that seemed good. It must be admitted, however, that the command to "subdue" the earth given to man in Genesis 1:28 has quite often been taken out of its biblical context and treated as an absolute license to do whatever we like. In the context of the Bible it has to be qualified (like the other mandates given to man before the Fall) by the restraints and the positive guidance of the Word of God for a *fallen* mankind. In the same verse man is commanded to "be fruitful and multiply, and fill the earth." No one treats the latter as an unqualified license for fallen men and women to have children indiscriminately. The sexual act is firmly placed within marriage as its only proper context. Here it is a great and enriching blessing; in any other context it is a deceitful and destructive evil. So also with the mandate to subdue the earth. For sinful humanity, it too must be set in the context of the wider biblical concern for care for others (including future generations) and respect for God's creation as something of real value not to be destroyed or expended lightly.

This context has been easily forgotten. In a largely secularized but so-called Christian culture, the exploitation of nature without respect to the effects has been all too common. Now the ecologists, including not a few Christians, have faced us with the consequences of such uncontrolled action. They have criticized what is going on, and some of their criticisms have to be accepted as Jethro-like warnings. At the same time we have to recognize that much of the ecology movement depends on a sort of romantic deification of nature. Nature is not sacred to the Christian. The natural environment is not perfect. Man is intended by God to gain his living from subduing nature to his use. We must be careful lest, in accepting certain criticisms, we overreact into a semipantheism that makes nature more important than it is in a Christian perspective. The ecologists may have jolted us into realizing that we have neglected truths, which are in fact biblical truths. We must not, however, be tricked into accepting their philosophy. Yet this has happened. Recognizing some truth in the environmental lobbies, Christians have been drawn into accepting the whole outlook, going overboard into a quite un-Christian emphasis on the issue, as if man had no mandate to farm natural resources. Abraham, when he accepted Pharaoh's entirely justified reproof of his deceit in saying that his wife was his sister (Gen. 12:10–20), was careful not to accept Pharaoh's paganism. Pharaoh, Jethro, and the ecologists speak some truths. We must listen to their advice and their criticisms, sift them, and accept what is in accordance with reality, even while we reject their overall outlook on life as quite misleading.

Wisdom and the Christian mind

Wisdom, therefore, is almost the same thing as a Christian mind. "Christ is our wisdom" and "we have the mind of Christ" come in the same passage. Wisdom is seen to have the same features as the Christian mind. It is first of all founded on God's revelation, and then it shows how to bring revealed truth to bear on practical issues. The chief thing that the study of wisdom adds to this discussion is the fact that unbelievers will be able to help us insofar as they see the real state of affairs of life. This explains Paul's remark in Titus 1 that what the pagan poet says "is true." Christian wisdom and the Christian mind must not despise knowledge from whatever source it comes. We must be critical and ask how far it is colored by the presuppositions of its proponents. But we must be willing to learn from non-Christians as well as Christians and to realize that a too theoretical

Christian approach in terms of Christian presuppositions may lack that humility that true wisdom must show. Our theological and philosophical pedigree may be faultless, but we may still be lacking in biblical wisdom if we are not close to the whole of Scripture *and to the whole of reality.* This relates to what is sometimes called "common grace." The term is unfortunate in several ways, and each author seems to define it differently. The concept, however, is useful. Non-Christians are not totally devoid of wisdom or of moral sense, and we must be deeply thankful to God for both the genuine learning and morality which many of them possess. They are able to discern the truth about life to a considerable extent and to be shrewd in applying those insights. It is part of God's goodness to all men (hence the term "common grace") that he enables them to understand and handle reality. It is in fact difficult to see how people could live in God's world at all if he had not made it possible for all men to understand it to a considerable degree, and this includes some moral understanding.

But consequently man can be held responsible for misuses of this knowledge. You cannot blame a man for not seeing things if he is totally blind; but you can blame him if, seeing things only faintly, he shuts his eyes and as a result breaks the furniture. The Old Testament blames the pagan nations for their gross pride and offenses against natural justice. God's people who do the same things are even more blameworthy. But the nations are not totally blind even to moral values. Abraham had to accept moral reproof from pagan kings (Pharaoh and Abimelech: Gen. 12 and 20).

The Christian, therefore, needs a greater humility than he sometimes shows in the face of the wisdom of human experience and learning. That is part of our true wisdom—to admit that we do not know things or understand the mechanisms of life as well as some other people do. That, however, in no way replaces the fact that the very beginning of wisdom is the fear of the Lord.

6

A Christian mind about man

Having tried to describe a Christian mind, and to distinguish it from other related ideas, I want in the remaining three chapters to explore its practical outworking in two ways. In this chapter I shall discuss a particular doctrine and some of its consequences. In the next two chapters I shall attempt a brief outworking in two major aspects of life. These can only be samples and, as I have already emphasized, I do not believe that a complete world-and-life view should be attempted as if such a system would have any finality or universal application. Readers from cultures other than my own will not necessarily think that the examples I have chosen are important, and they will certainly think of many things that I have left out. Here I start to explore some of the ways in which the Christian doctrine of man works out in different areas. I have chosen it partly because it is a doctrine where there is a sharp difference of view from that of the secular thinkers of today. It is also a doctrine that has very wide practical implications.

A Christian view of myself

If we follow the train of thought of Romans 12, the first application of all the great truths that Paul has set out in eleven chapters is, as we said, to my opinion of myself. Paul has highlighted three great truths in the Christian view of man. First, he stressed that man is a sinner, entirely unable to save himself and apparently hopelessly alienated from God and under God's judgment (chapters 1–3). He leaves us totally unable to claim any virtue or status before God. Our motives, even in our best moments, are mixed with evil; nothing has escaped our rebellious appetites for sin. "There is not health in us," as the Book of Common Prayer has it. Every aspect of man's character and life is infected by sin. We are spiritually dead, alienated from God and at enmity with God. No view of man could be more humiliating. We have absolutely no claim on God; and we cannot even say that we are better than others, because we are all failures by God's standards and fundamentally rebels.

Second, however, as soon as Paul has said that I am not to think of myself more highly than I ought to think, he adds, "but to think with sober judgment, each according to the measure of faith which God has assigned him" (Rom. 12:3). We "are one body in Christ, and individually members one of another. Having gifts . . . , let us use them" (vv. 5–6). The gospel shows us that we are the objects of God's love; and if that does not give us a hope, nothing else will. One of the great preachers of recent times used to say that when, first thing in the morning, he looked at himself in the mirror, hair disheveled, unshaven, unwashed, and not at all impressive, he would say to himself: "Do you know that you—astonishingly—are a child of God and an object of his love?" It was at the same time a humiliating and an elevating moment. This is the marvelous twin view of man described in Romans 3–5 which we are to apply to ourselves. Hopelessly lost in terms of our own resources and virtues, and yet rescued by the almost incredible generosity of God and restored to a place of honor and self-respect, we are actually part of the church, the body and bride of Christ!

In the third place, Romans 6–8 has set out a picture of life for those who are Christians that makes it plain that they are far from perfect as long as they are in this life, even though God offers us "all things that pertain to life and godliness" (2 Peter 1:3). Yes, we have the gift of the Holy Spirit, and he is transforming us progressively, giving us the mind of the Spirit rather than the mind of the "flesh" (Rom. 8:6-10). (Note again the contrast in terms of a change of our mind.) But while we are confident that one day he will complete his work, and that, meanwhile, in everything he works for good with those who love him (Rom. 8:28), we are as yet very imperfect. We do not always have a clear faith and we do not always live consistently, because evil is still present with us and in us. We are never to be complacent, therefore, about our state of character or our behavior. There is always a need to "grow in grace and knowledge"; there is always the possibility of evil erupting "out of the heart" and leading us into failure. Jesus stressed that evil comes from the heart and not from outside pressures (see Matt. 15:11 and James 1:13-14). Paul similarly warns us to beware just when we think we are secure; "let anyone who thinks that he stands," he says, "take heed lest he fall" (1 Cor. 10:12).

Probably all of us have heard of sad, and sometimes spectacular, failures of people whom we thought secure and strong Christians. It seems that it is often due to one of two things. On the one hand there is the temptation to allow "small" sins to continue without worrying about them: small dishonesties, small untruths, small affections for someone rather than the marriage partner, etc. On the other hand, there may be the kind of complacency against which these passages warn us explicitly. In 1 Corinthians 10 it is just when we are passing judgment on the failures of others that we need to be careful about ourselves. We must never be taken by surprise, then, when "out of our own hearts" arise unexpected, crude, and elementary temptations—things we thought we had long outgrown. If this were not true, it is hard to see why large tracts of the New Testament stressing mainly practical and ethical issues were necessary for the early church at all. They lived in something of a revival atmosphere, and we might have thought that they were too spiritual for these practical issues to be emphasized. This balance of the New Testament warns us that even at the height of religious enthusiasm and spiritual growth we must be vigilant, because the Devil is active and still finds within us a responsive chord.

Fourth, these three great themes in Romans are set against

an acceptance of man as a moral being, made in the image of God and still, even in his sinful state, showing many marks of that unique character. Romans takes this truth almost for granted. Other New Testament passages emphasize it more explicitly, as I hope to show later. It is easy to forget this if we are anxious not to underemphasize sin. But Romans 1 and 2 stress that man had both an awareness of God and a moral awareness, even before the law was known. It sees him as far different from, and more than, an animal. Man is capable of being blamed, and that speaks volumes for his dignity. Man is not just a product of his environment; neither is he just a complex machine. He has marvelous features that God have given by creation and preserved by providence. As the Book of Psalms frequently stresses, I am "fearfully and wonderfully made," am endowed with many noble characteristics so that, for instance, God's mercy can even be compared to a father's love: "As a father pities his children, so the LORD pities those who fear him" (Ps. 103:13). Indeed it is these virtues and abilities of man that make his sin so obnoxious and astonishing that we can hardly believe we are as deeply infected by it as we are. After all, is not man capable of noble thoughts and deeds? Yes he is, and that makes his sins stand out in even sharper relief and their pervasiveness all the more grievous. It must not make us try to pretend that man is not fallen.

Without such basic Christian views of man many wrong and conceited notions easily flourish. Equally, many unduly negative notions of ourselves may present themselves. The former danger is generally the greater because we are so self-satisfied. But both are serious because they leave us, in the first case, unguarded against evil and, in the second case, with such low morale that we never attempt great things for God. There is a school of psychology that tells people who are unreasonably worried about their faults that they can forget all about them because they don't really matter. This strange suggestion of deliberate suppression of truth seems, even in psychological terms, to be dangerous. In any case, the Christian does not need to run away from the worst aspects of his character and behavior, because he knows that there is grace for these faults. He can face them, as the non-Christian often cannot. He knows perfectly well that he cannot hide his faults from God, and so, because of God's offer of a totally free forgiveness that he does not have to try to earn, the sooner he comes into the open about them the better. A writer on psychological topics not long ago used to say that to have public confessions of sins in church was bad psychology and ought to be discontinued. Even if he had been up-to-date in his psychological theories, he failed to understand the quite different way in which the New Testament tackles the problem of sin. We can face the worst because we know the best.

Christian and humanist views of man

The Christian view of man is in these respects radically different from the humanist view of man generally prevailing in the West today. The view of man as basically sinful is, of course, unacceptable because of our pride; but it is also unacceptable to the humanist because he has no solutions to it. To be forced to admit, not only that other people are as bad as Christians assert, but that he is himself in that state, is often the first step toward taking seriously the remedies of which the Bible speaks. Several well-known humanists, such as W. H. Auden and C. E. M. Joad, started moving toward Christianity when they discovered that they were sinful at heart. This also seems to have been true of T. S. Eliot.

What is more, the humanist does not believe in a radical inner new birth or in spiritual resources to change our character progressively. Therefore he looks only for external forces to improve the admitted imperfections of people. A better environment, social life, or knowledge are the only remedies in this philosophy (except perhaps nowadays genetic engineering). Sex education in terms of mere information replaces moral education. While we are not to be negative about these external forces, and Christians must be (and have traditionally been) foremost in improving education, health, and social services, they cannot hope for these to do more than reduce the more socially obnoxious symptoms and results of sin. The humanist, therefore, tends to rely on social engineering and to treat sin as if it were merely a disease to be cured by social influences. While he believes in freedom, he cannot find a way to curb sin that does not risk Orwell's *1984*, methods which may involve the so-called treatment of criminals and, at their worst, putting dissidents into a mental hospital. So he tends to leave evil unrestrained, hoping that people will learn to control themselves sensibly.

The Christian believes in and experiences the transforming power of the grace of God in men's characters and the wide influence of Christian truth on man's outlook, even outside the church. Moral ideals based on true views of God and man can be influential for good even where people have no personal faith. Merely external ideals, however, cannot be influential for long, when the truths about God and man on which they rely are rejected. The Christian, therefore, puts a high value on both moral and religious education, believing that the truth has deeper influence than anything else. The humanist utopia turns out to be more parasitic upon residual Christian belief than appears at first sight. Few humanists are now happy with the actual results when society as a whole tries to live by a purely secular humanist ideal.

Nevertheless, while the Christian sees man as drastically fallen from what he was meant to be, he cannot regard him as "junk," to use Francis Schaeffer's vivid phrase. He has reason to respect all men, even the most insignificant, in a way that others cannot. Not long ago it was said that every single leprosy treatment center in the whole Indian subcontinent was of Christian origin. No one else had had a sufficiently high view of the individual, with the result that no one else had had an adequate reason for exerting himself greatly on behalf of those who were totally unable to make a contribution to society.

Further, the Christian believes that, when all allowances have been made for bad environments, men and women are still responsible beings to be treated with respect and, as such they are to be punished when they do avoidable evil. Because the Christian has such a high view of man, even in his sin, the Christian must insist that he is more than a malfunctioning machine due for servicing. He is a moral being who needs to be held to his moral responsibilities. This has far-reaching implications in social theory as well as for discipline in the home and the church. Heredity and environment shape character so that the forms of sin and our particular weaknesses and strengths are different. We may not be tempted at all to do some of the antisocial things that are an almost obsessive concern of others. But that does not mean that we are mere machines, and the Christian has to argue this insistently. Man is still created in the image of God, is still a responsible moral being capable of both good and evil, and this affects our social policy in fundamental ways.

The role of the state

This view of man explains in part the Christian view of the state which might otherwise appear to be an arbitrary and unrelated dogma. Romans 13 and 1 Peter 2 are the clearest passages and they tell us, among other things, that God has ordained the state to punish and restrain evil and to praise and encourage good. These functions make sense only if man is this extraordinary mixture of good and evil. There are social and personal virtues to be encouraged and praised. There are antisocial and personal evils that constantly break out, and they need not only to be restrained but also to be punished. Punishment is a means of upholding justice—particularly God's justice and his wrath at sin (Rom. 13:4). Those who have an almost entirely negative view of the state's role (i.e., to control sin) fail to realize that there are things in man that can respond to positive encouragement and that need that encouragement if they are to flourish (e.g., tax laws that assist giving to charities, and public recognition to "those who do well"). Those who do not believe in man's deeply fallen nature tend to avoid the biblical concept of punishment and to think of it purely as keeping the criminal locked up away from opportunities of further crime. (Incidentally, the Old Testament law provided for no prisons, but required compensation to those injured.) While seeking to cure him of his social illness, they tend to neglect the care of those he has injured or any concept of justice. The biblical view of man, by contrast, gives rational grounds for the role of the state and in particular tells why force may be needed to control man's evil.

Marriage and other sexual relationships

A Christian view of man has also a very practical bearing on our view of marriage. It relates in two main areas. First, it teaches us to regard marriage as a wonderful gift of God. It is a gift of creation that was first of all for partnership and friendship (Gen. 2:18). This means that we cannot regard it as sufficient that our marriage partner is a Christian. It is fundamental that he or she be that, and our partnership will be at best superficial, and at worst disastrous, without it. But marriage is a human relationship for this life—a gift of creation for our humanity. If it is the "beginning of marriage" that we both be Christians, it is not the whole of marriage by any means.

There is no marriage in heaven. Marriage was a gift before sin entered our human nature, and it continues to be a good gift for mankind today. Those who deny it, seeking to be "more spiritually minded," are described in 1 Timothy 4:1 as propagating a "doctrine of demons," presumably because that sort of denial of our humanity was part of many pagan cults and also spurns the excellence of God's wisdom and goodness in his creation order. Here some Victorian Protestantism departed a long way from a biblical ideal. Here, also, much Roman Catholic thinking has departed from the biblical ideal, and the Reformers were right to emphasize that according to the Bible, a married priesthood was better for most people than a celibate one. According to the New Testament, the gifts of God in creation for our humanity are not overthrown by grace, but rather transformed by it. Marriage, the family, the enjoyment of God's world are all seen as positively good gifts of creation to enjoy before God (see chapter 8). At the same time they are neither necessary, nor even the best, for some people. Each has his gift of God in this matter (see 1 Cor. 7), and in any case most people have a good many years of single life to enjoy also.

Quite apart from marriage, sexual differences must be seen as great and wonderful gifts of God's creation to be received with thanksgiving and lived out with joy under God's controlling guidelines. In the student world, many non-Christians envy the Christians their free and natural relationships between the sexes, relationships that depend on the fact that they respect and obey God's law. The pathetic comment of one male student—that he attended "gay parties" because there he could meet the girls on a natural basis, knowing that none of them wanted him to take them to bed after—illustrates the chaos to which the abandonment of God's law has brought people and the loss of freedom that that entails. We should always be deeply thankful that the law of God is good and health-giving and creates in our society relationships that are as good as can be achieved in a fallen world.

We have therefore to respect what our sexuality and marriage are meant to do for us on a human, this-worldly level. Marriage will not in itself be a spiritual blessing. It may enrich our fellowship with God and our prayer life and our Bible study if we share these things at an intimate level. But we can be too spiritual about it. It is also meant to minister to our loneliness, our self-centeredness, our emotional dryness, and our general welfare. If we fail to recognize that it is a *human* partnership first of all by creation, we may not realize what kind of partner we need or how we ourselves ought to contribute positively to the marriage. Not a few Christian marriages come under strain for this reason. The partners have forgotten its creation, its this-worldly nature, and therefore neglect one another. They also fail to enjoy fully God's blessings for our humanity and look only for the same kind of blessings that we receive in the church. Therefore they lose much.

Second, however, our view of ourselves and our partners as fallen human beings brings a warning that, even in the ideal marriage, neither of us is in fact an angel. It is right to have the highest ideals for marriage, but it is madness to believe that we shall be free from sin in the marriage relationship. Some Christian marriages seem to come to grief here. No sooner have unkind words been said or unloving actions done than people conclude that it is all over—my spouse cannot really love me, since someone who loved me could not have acted like that. But that is to forget that the partners are still sinners and that all sorts of horrible things can still come to the surface (or even be regularly on the surface until tamed by the gospel) in a way that is inconsistent with their true affection. A Christian who truly loves God can still be overcome by a quite inconsistent sin and probably still shows at times undeniable pride and selfishness, contrary though that is to a love for God. So also a true lover—because he or she is still a sinner—can still be overcome by inconsistent attitudes and deeds, even while there is really a deep continuing love for the partner. An analogy shows how to deal with the situation: we are to deal with it as God deals with our sins patiently and leads us on to greater Christlikeness. It is strangely difficult for many Christians to believe that they personally fail in this area. We believe that we sin in other areas, but we do not realize how far from angelic our attitudes, selfishness, and words and deeds seem to our partner, and how persistently we have to try to grow to be more like an angel!

A good marriage, therefore, needs to be built up all the time. We have to help one another in our own attitudes and actions. A friend whose marriage tragically fell apart after twenty years remarked that the basic fault was just that he had taken the marriage for granted and had not seen the need to be working at it all the time. Marriage should be a growing relationship (like our growth in Christlikeness of character) so that each year is better than the last. In neither area, however, does it come without effort. Those who think that a happy marriage will just happen, and that there will be no effort required, simply have not related the Christian doctrine of man to this area of life. Nevertheless, let us acknowledge the wonder of God's creative wisdom that built into marriage such marvelous features that two fundamentally selfish, individualistic, and sinful people can often be held together in a happy and constructive relationship for a whole lifetime! It is a marvelous achievement of God's goodness—with all the health-giving consequences to one another, to the children, and to society.

Education

The same fundamental truths about man apply in numerous ways to the education of our children and to education as a profession. We can consider only a few.

There is a sense in which, for the Christian, all education must be child-centered, because he sees each child as a unique creation of God and of personal value to him. Jesus constantly emphasized the value to God of "one of these little ones," and a variety of passages stress that we must respect every individual human being because he or she is made in the image of God (see, e.g., James 2:1–13). Our worth to God is one aspect of the doctrine of man which has far-reaching consequences in education. Yet when we are tired and the children are difficult or exuberantly active, it is easy to forget! A Christian attitude here contrasts with the Marxist and some other emphases that put the good of society so far above the good of the individual that the individual and the development of his created capacities can be readily brushed aside.

At the same time the Christian attitude to education contrasts with many idealistic theories holding that children are fundamentally good, needing only a good environment for the natural flowering of all social virtues. The Christian believes that children are both good and bad. There are fundamentally good features built in by creation, such as family affection, generosity, a sense of justice, a desire to love and to be loved, some moral awareness, an awareness of God—qualities which, if they develop, can blossom into magnificent adult virtues. At the same time, all these things are infected with evil so that there readily emerges selfishness, deviousness, delight in the downfall of others, hatred, jealousy, and the sort of self-seeking that happily turns a blind eye to moral values so as to climb over the less fortunate members of society. The parent or teacher is therefore faced, according to the Bible, with the need not only to encourage the good, but also to curb and discourage the evil. The moral law, we learn, is given to restrain evil (1 Tim. 1:8–11) by its authority and warnings. But there have been schools of thought that have taken a negative view of external discipline, either by parents or teachers. They have sometimes had an impressive academic pedigree and a foundation in the then-current state of opinion in educational philosophy and psychology. The Bible, however, contradicts them and values discipline. The Book of Proverbs says that wisdom leads us to reproof, correction, and punishment of offenders. The modern (i.e., late nineteenth century!) view of punishment is historically based on the idea that the human nature of children is basically good, needing only a better environment to fan its good features into flame and to discourage evil.

It is easy, however, for the Christian to see these as black and white alternatives, to overreact and to conclude merely that discipline in the school and home is a major duty. So indeed it is; but the accumulated wisdom of the child psychologists has very important points to make and has sometimes—Jethro-like— reproved Christians. The traditional Christian outlook has too easily been merely theoretical and, as a result, repressive. It has often forgotten Paul's command that parents should "not provoke their children" (Eph. 6:4; Col. 3:21). In Colossians, Paul gives a *psychological* reason for this: "lest they become discouraged." Many sermons have been preached on obedience to parents. Relatively few have been preached on these corresponding duties of parents to children. The child psychologists warn of the consequences of a repressive parental regime, even though, with nothing to guide them but psychology, they have failed to strike a right balance. What they say has to be criticized by the Bible, but we need to listen patiently for what truth they may have found.

Order, rules, and discipline in the home and the school are therefore seen by the Christian as needed restraints on evil. They are needed for "freedom-within-a-framework," which is the true Christian conception of freedom. The most agile animals have a skeleton which, by *restricting* the forces of muscular contraction, enables muscles to be used constructively. The painful process of practicing of music is necessary to be able to enjoy performing it. Similarly, in the moral field, "his service is perfect freedom." It is sometimes forgotten that throughout life one of the fruits of the Spirit is discipline. Of course discipline can be overdone, and the Bible has a marvelous balance. If only Victorian parents had remembered this, extremely happy Victorian families would have been more numerous and oppressive ones would at least have been deprived of an excuse in terms of Christianity.

The aims of Christian education could, therefore, be expressed as follows: To enable a child to develop the gifts and abilities that are his by creation and environment (including a grasp of spiritual realities) so that he can please God and serve the community. True personal fulfillment also comes this way, because that is the role for which we are created. It will be achieved only via discipline, because children are fallen. It will aim to serve society while never downstaging the individual.

If, then, we had to give a brief answer to a new teacher or school administrator, we should have to say something like the following. Do you see Christian guidelines for developing the gifts and abilities of pupils so that, even if they do not become Christians, they will serve their country, their families, and their colleagues well—as well as possible in accordance with their potential and a Christian scale of values? Is each child important to you because he is important to God, whether he is a Christian or not and whether he is very gifted or not? Do you care to develop such abilities as he has, even if he may never be grateful? Can you help him use them to serve society, even if not to serve God? If one of them is blind or academically backward, can you do as important a job for him as for the future Prime Minister? Your educational task is to be child-centered so that your students may be God-centered and live a life concerned to serve rather than to grab what they can.

This means, of course, that we cannot neglect moral education. Since the whole outlook of people and their aims in life are controlled to a large extent by their moral standards, that must have a very important place. Whether demanding moral standards can be maintained without religious conviction is a question that we cannot discuss here. It can be said, however, that the majority of those with strong moral convictions do find their strength in a religious faith and most of those who have very weak moral convictions have no religious faith. To fail to provide any means toward a religious faith, therefore, is often to fail to provide the means toward a strong morality and, as a result, to leave people without any constructive role in society. Certainly if we believe Christianity to be true, we want everybody to know about it and to know enough to be able to respond freely. We are not interested in indoctrination, which in any case does not make genuine Christians. We are interested in truth; and moral and religious truth are vastly more influential than other kinds of truth for people's fundamental ideals and motivation.

Life in society

In spite of all we have said about the importance of the individual in education, the Christian view of man also includes the view that he is intended to live in society: "It is not good that the man should be alone" was a primary reason for marriage. It is also one reason for the positive value that the Christian sets on family life. But it applies, in addition, to society as a whole. Indeed, in one passage Paul, in talking about society, makes the remark that "we are members one of another," and that has very far-reaching consequences.[1] As Paul goes on to say in that same passage, we are to aim to contribute to society and not to be parasites (Eph. 4:28). To equip someone for life in society may at first sight appear to be in conflict with the aim of personal growth and fulfillment. If, however, I am to be a good musician, sportsman, academician, politician, gardener, poet, etc., I have to develop certain gifts and set others aside. It is not physically

---

[1] The point in Ephesians 4:25 is why we should speak truth with our neighbor, i.e., with everyone. Those in the pietist tradition sometimes see this only as a reference to belonging together in the church and have missed an important point. They reduce the passage to an argument only for speaking truth to fellow Christians. This is clearly not the purpose of the passage, which is that we should speak truth with everyone because we all are members one of another in a broader sense. While in the church there is a unity in Christ which is referred to in similar terms elsewhere, it is true that, even in society as a whole, we are related in this way, and we owe truth to each other as one great feature of that bond. If truth is neglected it becomes a very different and much impoverished sort of society.

possible to be good at everything, and those who contribute most in their areas have often had to neglect other gifts for the sake of a few relevant ones.

That, however, is not a great privation, because the whole point of a society is that each contributes differently according to his ability. At its simplest level, the butcher, the baker, the candlestick maker each have a different part to play. Each can find satisfaction and joy in his role, even if he has at the same time to improve his gifts and his contribution. Here the Christian view of man cuts across those philosophies that see man's chief end simply in finding self-satisfaction or in doing his own thing. The New Testament tells us to aim above all to *serve* the community. Jesus told us to imitate his own example here and not to want to be one of those who orders others around or has a prestigious position (see Mark 10:42–45). This is a fundamentally different attitude to society from that which rules in many communities today, where the ideal is often the successful businessman, politician, or professional, and success is thought of principally in terms of money and a display of wealth and property. The Bible laughs at such "success." Jesus in one of his parables calls such people fools, and Psalm 2 tells us that "He who sits in the heavens laughs." One of the great tasks of education, therefore, is to help children develop an ideal of service, asking, "what can I put into life?" rather than "what can I get out of it?" We know that far greater satisfaction lies there than in the empty lives of so many highly "successful" people whose marriages and homes are a tragedy and to whom our Lord's words, "What does it profit a man, if he gains the whole world and loses or forfeits himself?" apply in the broadest way.

Man, animals, and the environment

The Christian view of man as made in the image of God, but fallen, also has wide-ranging consequences for an attitude to animals and to the whole of nature. According to the saying of Jesus himself, and in accord with the creation mandate given to man in Genesis 1:28, man is "of more value than many sparrows." Although man must respect the whole of nature because it is such a wonderful creation of God, he is at the same time given a position and responsibility of stewardship over it. The animals are in the biblical view not our brothers. Men are made in the image of God, and much modern talk about the natural order, as if animals had rights comparable to those of man, or as if the preservation of wilderness was in itself something sacred, is contrary to the Christian emphasis. Of course, the Christian view of the creation mandate can be secularized and abused. But to accuse Christians of being responsible for spoiling the environment is really nonsense. It is when we forget that the whole created order deserves our respect because it is created by God, and then alone, that we are likely to misuse it.

The point here is that, to many environmentalists, man is no longer seen as God's vice-regent and steward of the world. He is in their view put under nature with a duty to preserve it as "sacred," not over it with a duty to cultivate it for God and for mankind. The Christian doctrine of man's status and his God-given task in the world are crucial to any positive view of science and of culture generally (see also chapter 8). The need for a positive view does not prove, of course, that it is right. The Christian contention, however, is that we are given such a positive view of man's role. There is something wrong from a biblical point of view in setting the simple rural life as an ideal to which we should seek to return. Also, as anyone knows who lives a rural life, it is just as much plagued by human sin as is the city and its technology. Some writers speak as if they want to return to subsistence farming—or its urban equivalent. They forget that that kind of life is dependent on science and technology if it is to enjoy a clean and adequate water supply, health services, balanced diet, education, great music, the ability to visit relatives and friends, etc.

In any case, farmland such as we enjoy in most of the developed countries is a very different thing from the "natural" environment of dense woods (complete with wolves, bears, rats, mosquitoes, indigenous typhoid, malaria, cholera, and plague) which covered most of the land before men started creating farms, clearing hills for grazing, draining marshland, etc. It is good that such natural environments should not be completely destroyed. They are part of our heritage. But none of us really thinks that everyone should live in a mud-and-wattle hut with only swamp water to drink and wild animals and fruit for food. The rural life looks attractive only if it has all the modern conveniences of a shop around the corner, a telephone to call a doctor in an emergency, and preferably flush toilets, penicillin, and kerosene or gas for lamps. There is a proper protest against luxury and extravagance, which are also attacked in the Bible, especially when they are at the expense of others. But there is no value in setting aside God-given abilities to improve our health and welfare or in reverting to some romantic ideal of the "natural." Nature also is not perfect and needs to be improved.

This chapter has presented a number of examples. Even the most obvious things, however, are brought into doubt today, partly because people do not know the nature of man. I have been glad on more than one occasion to speak in a university debate on a motion such as "that the Christian view of man alone does justice to the facts." One of the impressive results of such a discussion has been to see just how unconvincing are the alternatives when the advocates have to defend them. In one area after another one can stress that the biblical doctrine of man and the conclusions that can be drawn from it do fit reality and give guidelines for life that cannot be matched by any other view. This should make us all the more determined to clarify and to hang on to a Christian view even in areas where the immediate results of doing so may *not* be clear or immediately convincing. A Christian is convinced that God's Word is given for sinful man. Christian ethics are tailor-made for fallen man and relate to man as he is. Therefore we must not weaken when a particular Christian position is thought to be difficult to defend on psychological or sociological grounds. God's psychology and sociology are better than ours.

The Christian view of man provides a sure basis that justifies much in the Christian life. Without that view of man Christian ethical commands may seem arbitrary or irrational to the humanist, but, as John says of Jesus, "He knew what was in man."

7

Work, the job, and unemployment

One of the places where the difference between a Christian and a non-Christian outlook is seen most clearly is in the attitude to work. Judging by what they say, many people now regard work simply as an unfortunate, but necessary, evil. The less you have to do, the better, and what cannot be avoided is done looking forward to the holidays, weekends, or retirement. Until recently the ideal society has been presented by many as one in which machines will eventually take over every work function, so enabling men and women to enjoy almost unlimited leisure.

This is a romantic ideal that comes partly from the enthusiasm of the romantic poets and other thinkers who expected to find freedom in a totally spontaneous life uncontrolled by the hard realities of the material world. The theoretical "noble savage" who manages to live a life of leisure with a bit of enjoyable hunting for food, or the cultured intellectual who lives by his not too strenuous music or philosophy, were the ideal. This has overtones of a Greek or otherwise pagan idolization of the intellectual, emotional, and aesthetic life as against manual or other physically exhausting work. It still has an appeal, partly because of our natural laziness, but also partly because of a justified impression that many jobs are boring, especially much factory work of a mass production kind which is undoubtedly deadening and dehumanizing. In fact, a whole group of not closely related factors has combined to build up a negative view of work as something to be avoided if at all possible. Perhaps this is a large part of what was meant in Genesis 3 when, following the entrance of sin into the world, man was told that from then onward work would be tiresome and even painful to him.

Now, however, we have discovered that the answer is not quite so simple. Retired people also have great problems dealing with boredom and find it difficult to discover a sense of worthwhileness. The unemployed find life at home even more boring than life at the factory and experience great psychological as well as social and material difficulty. Early retirement is far from popular for people who cannot see a useful task in the years ahead. When working hours are shortened beyond a certain level people look around for another part-time job to fill the gap. Work is in fact anything but dehumanizing in itself. People seem to like work and find it therapeutic—at least up to certain levels.

Work as a creation ordinance

The Christian perspective on this, which alone explains the situation adequately, is often forgotten. According to the Bible, work was part of man's ideal life even before the Fall. He was charged in Genesis 1:28 to subdue the earth, and in Genesis 2:15 he was given the task of gardening or farming. The Old Testament frequently refers to the rewards of work as a source of joy and satisfaction to men and women. The ideal wife of Proverbs 31 is not a lady of leisure, but is very busy indeed, sometimes into the small hours of the morning. The New Testament tells us that we are to work so that we may put more into life than we take out of it (see below, and Eph. 4:28).

The Fall only altered this ideal insofar as it made work burdensome and more demanding. In Genesis 3:17–19 it is said, "In toil [or painful toil] you shall eat of it [the ground]," and "in the sweat of your face you shall eat bread." The Creation ordinance of work as a part of the very good world remains. Work, a Christian believes, is a benefit to man, spoiled only to some extent by sin. Our aim is not to abolish it, but to make it serve its true purposes.

Further, the Bible never accepts the Greek exaltation of intellectual or artistic work over the manual. One of the results of the rediscovery of the Bible at the Reformation was the realization that manual work was as worthy an occupation for the Christian as the more intellectual occupations. Gardening or carpentry (was not Jesus a carpenter?) is as honorable as composing music or writing philosophical books. Value is not found merely in manual work as some believe; neither is it found merely in intellectual work as others have argued in the past. To the Christian, manual and intellectual work are of equal worth.

As Christians we find ourselves today having to defend our position against attacks on two fronts. Against those who make work an idol, we have to say that it is merely one means of serving God and man. Against those who regard work as a necessary evil, we have to stress that, by Creation, man is in fact meant to be at work in the world, turning its natural resources and the gifts of human nature to the good of the community. The Christian believes, therefore, that a workload of reasonable proportions is in fact God's intention and something that serves man's health and well-being. At the same time, Christians have often been foremost in attacking the excessive workload that has been placed on employees by those who control the work processes. It was necessary to create labor unions and to bring in legislation to limit working hours—especially for children. The Christian ideal is neither the workaholic who lives for his work nor the person who has very little work to do.

The old question, "When Adam delved and Eve span, Who was then a gentleman?" which goes back to the fourteenth century, still has its point. Adam was not a "gentleman" in the terms of that non-Christian ideal of idleness. The gentleman of leisure is not a Christian model, and we should not aspire to it. The biblical ideal is the man who can sit under his own vine and his own fig tree and enjoy their fruits—which do not come without considerable, ongoing work week after week. The Christian wants a balance of work and recreation.

Astonishingly, the negative view of work is still very

widespread today. Even some career counselors have been infected with it and encourage people to try to live on as little work as possible. This is probably the result of long decades of the fight to reduce working hours and to improve conditions compared with those that ruled in the early days of the Industrial Revolution. The pendulum has swung too far, however, and now we are discovering on a grand scale that the idle, whether forced or unforced, are not really to be envied at all. Many of them are exceedingly miserable—in spite of the false picture given to us by the TV concept of the idle rich and their "good life." The man who can live comfortably without a job is in fact happy only if he has some interesting, and usually socially useful, tasks to do. Most people want to feel that they have accomplished something by their own efforts, and most would like that to be also socially useful.

Of course, the idle rich profess to be happy, and it is not our primary duty to call their bluff. What Christians want to say is that living as God has made us to live leads to far greater health and well-being. That includes what Paul in Ephesians calls "doing honest work" for a not negligible part of our week. It was never the ideal to work a seven-day week. By Creation there is to be one whole day of rest in seven, as well as rest in each twenty-four hours. But some work, especially work that serves to "subdue the earth" to man's needs, is a richly rewarding part of the normal and ideal life of man in the Christian view.

This stress on work that will help to "subdue the earth" so as to develop its resources and the resources of human nature, such as our artistic and technical abilities, can, however, be made too austere. There is certainly great satisfaction in achieving something that gives health, wealth, and happiness to others, and we are meant to enjoy that. But God has made work in itself a pleasure when it is not excessive. We are so made that we find enjoyment in using our gifts. This is part of the Creation order. A famous international singer, Janet Baker, told us in recent interviews that, while she regarded her voice as a great gift and therefore a great responsibility to use for others, it was only in later life that she realized that it was also proper for her to enjoy its use wholeheartedly and to find deep pleasure in singing well. That discovery, she believed, improved her singing—as one might expect. Man is not only to do work, but also to enjoy it. The result of sin is that it has become burdensome or even painful when it should not be so, and one result of a Christian attitude to work is that a good deal of the sting is taken out of it, and work is done with a new pleasure.

At the same time, of course, the Christian cannot live for his work. Work can so easily become an idol, and that is a terrible distortion of a truly Christian view. Some people drive themselves into a breakdown in order to reach the top when they are not really capable of it. Others never realize their potential because they are too lazy or inadequately motivated. The Christian wants to find the point between the two where he has real satisfaction in fulfilling his responsibilities to work hard and well and so to make a real contribution to life, while at the same time he remembers that he is far more than a mere "role" in society. Success is not his god; God has given him other responsibilities and roles as well. It is important that he fulfill his responsibility to God, the family, neighbors, friends, colleagues at work, the state, as well as that he excel in some gifts. He cannot be a mere "organization man."

Some years ago I met a distinguished scientist and asked him a little humorously when he was going to be made a Fellow of the Royal Society (FRS). He answered that he expected a man under him to get the FRS before he achieved it—if he ever did. That man had sold himself to his job. His marriage was breaking up under the strain, but he was doing outstanding work. My friend saw his responsibility as being to keep a balance. He had recently, after very careful thought and prayer, agreed to become an elder in his church. He believed he was doing justice to his professional work, though many of his research papers would appear with his research students' names first and not under his name alone. He had to think of his wife and family, etc. It turned out as he said. The man under him got an FRS quite soon. But he himself was similarly recognized not many years after, so he can hardly have been neglecting his gifts!

This attitude to work does mean that, in some occupations, not many Christians rise to the very top. They have instead a way of forming a solid backbone in their profession or business. When they *are* found among the leaders, especially in science and medicine where some have been quite outstanding, it is often due to the originality of their thinking rather than to sheer overwork. But because they often provide a reliable core in their profession or business and, in so doing, do much to shape its ideals and codes of practice, Christians have often been more influential than they may realize. The fact that they have not established for themselves an international reputation, often much sought after by their colleagues, is something they are happy to accept, where such a position can be reached only by making an idol of one's work. Neither money nor personal success is the thing they live for.

Motives for work

The New Testament explains how a Christian attitude can be maintained. Perhaps the best-developed example is in Ephesians 6:5–9 where Paul addresses both slaves and masters, applying all that he has said to the former equally to the latter with the phrase, "Do the same to them." Paul first of all addresses slaves who had no choice of work and among other tasks did all the least interesting and most unpleasant jobs. (He is not here talking to people who have got into the profession of their choice!) To them he says that they are to do their work "with fear and trembling" (when compared with the same phrase in 1 Corinthians 2:3, this seems to mean with a sense of serious responsibility lest we fail), "in singleness of heart" (i.e., whole-heartedly) and "as to Christ." His point here is that slaves are to serve *as if* they had been ordered to their jobs by Christ himself and not by their earthly masters. Their spirit and attitude in their work is to be as it would be if Christ were their supervisor. They cannot be time-watching or skimping or currying favor, but rather they must try to do the job well.

Paul's next point then reinforces this. The slave is "doing the will of God. . . , rendering service." This is different from the "as to Christ" of the previous verse. It states that, in doing work which serves people, even if they do not deserve it, we are in fact doing the will of God.

This is a very important point. It implies that God cares for the work itself. It matters to God that the needs of the household or farm, etc., be met. We can, therefore, take a double interest in our work, however unpalatable it is in itself. We do it "as if" Christ had told us to, and we want to do his bidding. We do it also knowing that it serves the community, and that God values this and has ordained such work for the good of man. Cleaning the lavatory is therefore to be done enthusiastically!

That enthusiasm is Paul's next point. Such work is to be done "from the heart, rendering service with a good will as to the Lord and not to men." The Christian is, then, to develop a Christian mind about his work whatever it is, so that he does it enthusiastically. It may not be the kind of work he wants to do or is trained to do; but if it is at all useful to anyone he can do it with joy. This exposes one of our problems today. I have been concerned that some Christians who, in a tough employment situation, end up in a job far from their ideals, are constantly grumbling about it. What would they say if they were slaves? To grumble here is to express two faults—a failure of a Christian mind about work and a failure of trust in God's providence for his children. A very experienced missionary administrator once commented to me that when missionaries began to grumble it was a very serious danger signal. He expected them soon to have to give up their work and to come home permanently, because there was a failure of faith that God for a good reason had put them where they were and that with God they could turn all the problems to his glory. It must often have been similar with slaves. Indeed grumbling is mentioned several times in the New Testament as a serious fault along with much more blatant evils. Typically Paul has not only told the slaves not to grumble or to work grudgingly; he has gone beyond that to a whole doctrine of work which enables them to do it from their heart and with a thought-out Christian attitude to work. A mere exhortation to work cheerfully would never have achieved that for most of us.

Finally, Paul in this passage says that we are not to work "as men-pleasers" but to remember the divine reward (v. 8). That is to say, we are to work neither for the paycheck nor for status. Our motivation is to be the better one of working for the Lord and receiving his rewards. This overthrows the only motive for working hard that remains to many non-Christians. Christians can all too easily fall into working for pay, profit in business, or success and status, but that is to descend to a non-Christian outlook. Slaves, of course, were not actually paid; but their situation could be improved by currying favor with the boss. We are extremely easily trapped into working for similar materialistic motives.

In history there is little doubt that the Christian motives described in this passage have been far more powerful than financial inducements. Governments think that they can stimulate hard work merely by lower taxes, more financial incentives, and promoting the image of the successful person. It may have a limited effect; but the readoption of a Christian mind on work that was widespread a hundred years ago would be vastly more effective. At the same time it would be much more likely to promote industrial cooperation rather than conflict. Motivation merely by financial gain is not God's way and does not promote his kind of society, even if it can get work done. The motives that God commands, as in so many other ethical areas, have a wide-ranging effect for good if they are put into practice. They deal with a particular issue, but they also help in many other areas besides. (I am not here entering into what may be politically expedient when Christian motivation is weak, nor the question of the place of profit in a business.)

This is not to say that the profit motive can be totally eliminated. Many societies that have tried to replace peasant farming by communal farming have discovered this to their cost. If harder work than the minimum is to bring no material reward, then the long hours and extra work that a family will do on the land for their own benefit will rarely be done for the communal benefit. It is no good being too idealistic here. Without encouraging covetousness, we have to accept that many people need some element of personal gain to motivate them to go above the minimum workload. This is particularly true when they are really poor and the extra is wanted in order to give a healthy life to the family. This has nothing to do with capitalism or socialism. While capitalism has sometimes tended in practice to encourage covetousness, even at the expense of others, socialism has tended to leave people in poverty longer than necessary, because it has failed to recognize that sheer idealism will not usually be enough to produce the goods. There is a kind of self-seeking which, especially in poor countries, cannot be dismissed as covetousness, but is a sensible and worthy effort to make better use of the resources God has given us for ourselves and our families. Society can harness this kind of self-seeking, which does no harm to anybody else, for the communal good. It can raise the standard of living and help to make the country self-sufficient in food. The same applies to tasks other than agriculture. While personal gain can easily get out of control, the aim to build up an enterprise so as to create wealth, jobs, and commodities for the community can be a worthy Christian motive, so long as the method of doing so is also acceptable.

The Protestant work ethic

There is, of course, an enormous literature about the "Protestant Work Ethic" (PWE), starting with the famous thesis of Max Weber in 1904–1905. As a recent review of the literature has shown,[1] this is far from being a simple discussion, and several of the writers concerned did not have an adequate understanding of the theological issues when they tried to describe past influences. We are not here concerned with the relation of the PWE to capitalism, and in any case it would need an expert to walk through that minefield surefootedly. There are, however, some things that we can say with confidence about a biblical work ethic. In any so-called Christian culture the truly biblical emphases will always be mixed up with their secularized versions. That one should regard hard work as a virtue, for instance, may be a view sincerely held by some on a Christian basis. But in the same community, when it is seen to produce

---

[1] W. Stanford Reid in *Themelios*, vol. 8, no. 2, 1983.

prosperity, there will be plenty of other inadequate or false motives put up alongside genuinely Christian ones. If the community still uses a lot of religious language, some of these will be dressed up in a Christian form. Thus, Weber stressed the motive of "working out our election" in and through our job, but it is doubtful how important this ever was to biblical Christians. R. H. Tawney also seems to fail to grasp some of the key aspects of a biblical emphasis and attributes to the PWE motives that are nearer to a Roman Catholic understanding of the place of "works." One has to be critical of much of the supposed bases of the PWE in the literature, because it is not really Protestant.

The rediscovery of the Bible at the Reformation, however, did certainly inject some new emphases into the situation, and the rapid development of business, as well as the rise of science and technology over the same period, owe much to these fresh emphases. One of these is undoubtedly the emphasis in the Ephesians 6 passage and elsewhere in the New Testament where there is *explicit* teaching about work. Work is to be done not only as if for Christ, but in the consciousness that we are actually pleasing God in subduing his world for the service of mankind. God in this view actually cares. The rediscovery of this understanding of work had a deep effect at the Reformation. It led on to the view that any job could be a vocation—a calling from God himself. The humblest job was immediately lifted to a new level and could be done with a new enthusiasm because God cared about it and had given us this task. George Herbert's seventeenth-century hymn expresses the biblical view that work is to be done "for thy sake":

A servant with this clause
  Makes drudgery divine:
Who sweeps a room, as for thy laws,
  Makes that and the action fine.

The fact that a poet spoke like this is significant. The point was understood at a popular level. Everyone agrees that this new concept of vocation contrasts sharply with the pre-Reformation emphasis when only the "spiritual" tasks of the church were a vocation. We must ask ourselves whether we have lost these biblical emphases on service and vocation, and, if so, we must try hard to recover them.

At the same time, there is one great contrast between our situation and that at the rise of Protestantism. The Protestant emphasis on work contrasted with the ascetic ideal of the pre-Reformation church. Today we are chiefly confronted with a materialistic view of work—capitalist, socialist, and Marxist. While we must not go back to a negative view, we have to fight even harder against the new materialistic bias which approaches work from a different angle from that of pre-Reformation thinkers, emphasizing chiefly its economic (or personal gain) aspects. Christians are now in greater danger of making profit or moneymaking their ideal, because that is the view of so many people around us. It is not for nothing that the Bible has frequent warnings against covetousness and materialism and that 1 John concludes with the cryptic words, "Little children, keep yourselves from idols."

A Christian view of things

This rediscovery of work as a vocation went along with the rediscovery of the Bible's emphasis on the material world as a gift to man from God and a sphere of God's concern. He is interested not only in our souls but also in our bodies (see Matt. 6:25–34). He and his disciples healed as well as preached. He cares that natural resources are well used for mankind for our this-worldly comfort and health (see the next chapter).

While in previous ages the "natural" had been regarded as sacred and it was felt to be wrong to interfere with it, it was seen that the Bible encourages us to treat all creation as God's good gift to men to be used responsibly in our service. It was no longer even ungodly to experiment on nature. This was a mandate not to exploit the earth, but to develop its resources, as a man may seek to use the resources of the building lot he expects to occupy for decades and to pass on to his children. It was, as we said in the previous chapter, *stewardship* for mankind and also a stewardship from God, since all resources are his. The land and its possibilities (like work and its possibilities) were to be used as a service to God and men. God was believed to be interested that we should make good use of all the great resources that are at our disposal in his creation. From this came an entirely fresh stimulus to science and technology that was able to find delight in "thinking God's thoughts after him" (by discovering how wonderfully the world is made), and at the same time to be thankful in using its resources for human benefit. The early members of the Royal Society were largely people of a Puritan outlook. It has been calculated that 80 percent of the early members held a Puritan theology, even if they were not necessarily personal Christians. As late as the middle of the nineteenth century Psalm 111:2 was a text for scientific research: "Great are the works of the LORD, studied by all who have pleasure in them." Lord Rutherford had them written over the door of his laboratory at Cambridge where some of the greatest advances in physics took place. They still stand there, though unfortunately in Latin so that not everybody knows what they mean!

In much of the literature about the so-called Protestant work ethic, this point has been missed. It is not only a Christian view of *work* that characterized the biblical reemphasis that followed the Reformation, but especially in the more Calvinist tradition (whether it was called that or not), the positive Christian view of *things* had a crucial part to play. The result was not only a new attitude to work and business activity, but a new attitude to science and technology. This stood in contrast to those who thought that the contemplative life or the Christian ministry were the only real vocations, and thus it put new meaning into "sweeping a room"—and, incidentally, made a major contribution toward the growth of democracy.

We could say, then, that the most important impact of a Christian mind on the whole subject of work is that the priority is changed from an emphasis on rewards to the ideal of service. If that does not describe my attitude to work, then something is seriously wrong.

The job

The practical outworking of all this is important. Does it matter whether I teach math well or not, so long as I run a good Inter-Varsity Christian Fellowship chapter in my spare time? Does it matter to me as a Christian how I work in business or as a manufacturer, so long as I evangelize my colleagues or employees? Does it matter whether I am a good bank clerk, accountant, or civil servant, so long as I am honest, keep my faith, and fulfill my duty within the church?

The biblical answer to all these questions is undoubtedly, "Yes, it does matter." It matters to God and therefore it must matter to me. It is part of God's plan for mankind that we should learn how the world works so that we can use its resources. It is part of God's plan that the products of these resources should be available as widely as possible so that everyone should have the benefits of God's world at as low a cost as possible. It is pleasing to God that we do our work at the desk or the bench in such a way that we have done it for Christ himself and are glad to offer it to him as a piece of service.

There are, of course, a few occupations for which the Christian can have no enthusiasm. It is doubtful whether he should be enthusiastic to develop an industry that makes entirely unnecessary luxuries or products that are harmful to most of the users. Only if in conscience a man is satisfied that tobacco is a benefit to a substantial proportion of its users (for relaxation, or as an escape from worse drugs) could he be able to be in the tobacco industry with the sort of positive enthusiasm that Ephesians 6 requires—unless he is "a slave of circumstances" who has no option. He could not produce pornography as a service to Christ; but he could do most of the activities of our society in that way, because most of them do minister to the this-worldly good of man and help to fulfill the creation mandate.

If this seems obvious, I can only say that it is not obvious to everyone. There is still a sneaking suspicion that you could not, or should not, be positive about many occupations that are not only wholesome but very useful. A religion teacher recently expressed to me severe reservations about encouraging people to go into business. He was obviously keen to get people to understand Christianity. Somehow he could not see that his pupils should also take pleasure in producing the bicycle, car, or bus by which he traveled to school each day, the class textbooks, the school buildings, the furniture, food, or soap in his home. By contrast, a Christian electronics engineer in business told me that he felt a real sense of achievement that a radio which cost ten dollars in the 1930s still costs only ten dollars today in spite of inflation and is, therefore, within the reach of a far wider circle of society. He felt his industry had done something useful in achieving this result. That latter attitude seems to me to be fundamentally Christian, while the religion teacher's attitude is not.

To take another example: I recently met a computer programmer who had become a Christian only a few years before. He told me that he was thinking of giving up his job because he could not see that it benefited anyone and was only increasing the gap between rich and poor countries. He had no positive idea of what he could do instead, merely a vague uneasiness about his job. When pressed, he told me that it was because he had been reading certain literature based on a more or less Protestant ascetic tradition. This seemed to have keyed in with his Catholic background to have left him with an almost total lack of enthusiasm for any job in industry. Yet it should have been possible on biblical grounds for him to be intensely positive about it. His very right concern for the gap between rich and poor countries would not be served by the decline in ability of the richer countries to buy from the poorer ones. Of course there are jobs that can involve exploitation of others, and the Christian must be willing to stand against that in his firm and to risk losing his job as a result. Perhaps there are whole industries that are exploitative. But one has to ask which is the better alternative, to fail to buy from the poor countries or to buy at a price that is not unfair? If the richer countries are to do the latter, then a healthy economy is essential. As we have seen in recent years, a serious decline in the richer countries has very soon led to a further decline in the poorer ones. It has not led to the redistribution of wealth. If my friend had had a healthy, positive view of the value of material well-being, then he should have seen that doing any constructive job well would be serving others and that he could do it with enthusiasm as something that was doing the will of God.

Unemployment

If work is one of the Creation ordinances and is for man's health and welfare, what can we say about the unemployment that is a worldwide phenomenon today? First, let it be said that *paid* work is not the only form of work. The housewife's role, for instance, is in a biblical perspective every bit as honorable as any paid job and more important to society than most of them. It is not at all clear, therefore, that households with children at home where both parents go out to paid jobs have always got their priorities right. At the same time paid work provides people with key supports, and their loss is a serious deprivation for most people. Interestingly, the loss of money is rarely the main problem in any country where the welfare services do not leave the unemployed in abject poverty.

1. The job gives a community of fellow-workers. Here we belong to a subculture and have the dignity of being a member of that community as well as the stimulus of their companionship. Those who have ever had a job feel this loss most acutely.

2. The unemployed have too much time on their hands and therefore suffer the debilitating effects of boredom, lack of stimulus, and often lack of any organization and structure in life. In spite of all the grumbles, it is good to have a timetable, some clear working hours, something that requires our thought or our physical action. Even very routine jobs are almost always preferred to unemployment. Like children who ask lugubriously, "What shall I do," adults find idleness very difficult. And as with children, of course, there is also the invitation to mischief.

3. There is a loss of identity—especially a loss of status—which is reinforced by the shortage of money. We not only do not have the secondary identity of being the teacher, accountant, or factory worker, we also lack the money to go out and

about and entertain and enjoy some of the things that others enjoy.

4. From a Christian point of view one of the most important aspects for most people is the lack of any sense of usefulness. Most non-Christians share with Christians the desire to feel useful. To be unemployed makes them feel dependent on society. They would like to be making a positive contribution, and they feel they are not doing so.

There are other factors, but these four items alone can be a formidable deprivation. They are especially aggravated when others, and most of all others in the family or the church, seem to look down on the unemployed. They are easily given the impression that they are in some sense a failure to be treated with a kindly but patronizing outlook. The result slides over into a devastating loss of self-respect and the collapse of any motivation to exert themselves. In turn this leads easily to depression or anger against society.

If this analysis is at all correct, then what we have said above about work is very relevant. It means that the church must first of all honor and care for the unemployed as they do for someone who has just suffered an accident or bereavement. Their loss of social status and finance should be no loss of status with us. We should encourage them and help them to get on their feet again as quickly as possible. They should know that their place in the church is as much respected as that of the successful business-man or professional (see James 2). We must not be snobs about jobs.

Secondly, we most put at their disposal all the resources of the church fellowship to help them overcome their difficulties so that they do not lose either proper self-respect or motivation to exert themselves to serve others. Opportunities for this should be thought out and put before them. This has been done in a very successful way in many churches.

On the other side, however, it is not helpful to do too much for them; they rightly want to take the initiative for themselves, and they must be encouraged to do so if they are sliding into a position of undue dependency. Social deprivation, like personal loss of any kind, can be used to promote personal growth if it is tackled in the right way. Indeed it may be that being leaders in a group of unemployed people could give that kind of stimulus to develop their gifts that a paid job might not have given them. That does not make the loss a good thing but the church must try to turn it to good.

Finally, unpaid work is from a Christian point of view just as valid an outworking of the Christian mandate as paid work. There is, therefore, need to help one another to find ways of doing useful things, and above all serving the community with the new resources of massive spare time. It is not easy to work it out if part of each day is spent in the search for paid jobs, but again it has been done very successfully in some churches, and the Christian perspective on work means that this is just as valuable as a job.

This, of course, is not to suggest that we do not try to tackle the broader problems that leave so many people without any apparently worthwhile work to do. There are political, economic, and social factors on a wide scale that must also be of concern to us, and the Christian may need to speak up about Christian priorities in this area. But even if we cannot change the political scene in a hurry, the Christian attitude to work can accomplish much on the small scale. It can give the unemployed a new perspective on their situation and positive aims for the use of their time and energies apart from looking for a job.

Some practical conclusions

What practical results does this discussion lead to? I suggest the following:

1. All Christians ought to find a role in society in which they help to increase the resources of the community. They do not want to be merely a drain on others if they can help it. They want to serve God by serving men. That is the primary Christian motive for work of any kind—farming, business, professional life, homemaking, or construction work. We need to ask ourselves whether that is our attitude to our future or present job (see Acts 20:34–35). Service, not profit, is the Christian's first motive. To reverse that order is paganism.

2. To the Christian it is not fundamentally relevant whether this is a paid or unpaid job. Those who have no home responsibility and for whom no paid job is available are therefore to look for ways of being useful in an unpaid capacity. This is surely as true of retired Christians as of people who are unemployed. We will only want to be sure that we are not depriving other people of paid work.

3. Service to our own families has a very high priority in the New Testament. Biblically this includes the elderly as well as children. Next comes the church family and then all those around us whom we might be able to serve.

4. We must not allow our own desire for a standard of living above what is necessary to distort our Christian aims and priorities. We need often to question our motives when we seek higher earnings (see 1 Tim. 6:6–10).

5. We should be able to do our work with enthusiasm. If the job we have trained for and hope for is not available, we must learn to go into something else with gusto. There are too many people who should be thankful to have any paid job at all, yet who spend the time grumbling that it is not the ideal job of their choice. Slaves had no choice; and over the centuries many ordinary working people have had effectively no choice as to what they did.

6. Such an attitude would be hard for the non-Christian to maintain. But the Christian who believes in God's sovereignty and sees the most menial task as service to his Lord ought to be able to find it much easier and to find satisfaction and joy in doing his job as well as he can, even though he may at the same time seek ways of serving that are more in line with his gifts. This seems to have been the specific teaching of 1 Corinthians 7:21 about slaves. He should do the job while at the same time, if he is given the opportunity of being free, he should take it.

7. We should therefore be greatly concerned to be good at our job and not only, or chiefly, because this may bring promotion, money, or a good reputation. We believe that God is concerned that all the resources of the world be increasingly well used. Most jobs contribute to this, and according to our ability we should take the opportunities of service wholeheartedly.

Whether we go into Christian ministry or other forms of direct Christian witness or whether a good deal of our Christian witness is in and through our job is a matter of gift from God. There is nothing more spiritual in being a minister or missionary than in being a factory worker. It is just a question of what abilities God has given us and what he wants us to do. There may be some occupations in which it is more difficult to be honest than in others; but that is no reason for the Christian to run away or to feel that it is spiritual to go into the jobs where it is easy.

8. This overall positive view of our job as service to God through service to the community is very much needed at the present time. We need to bring it to bear on every activity and to help one another never to be ashamed of what we are doing so long as it is something that we can do with a good conscience in the way we have discussed. The unemployed should be able to lift up their heads and say that at the moment they have no paid job, though they are looking for one; but they have found some jobs to be done in the meantime in which they find joy and satisfaction in serving the Lord and their fellowmen. Meanwhile, we seek also to serve others in our spare time, whether that is very little or too much. There is plenty to do.

8

A Christian view
of culture

Christian views of culture have an enormous influence over many questions in the church and in personal life. Like Christian views of work, however, they have varied considerably over the history of the church. When the church has been a small minority in a strongly alien culture, Christians have tended to seize on the more negative statements in the Bible and to adopt the view that we must separate ourselves entirely from the world's culture. When the church has been stronger, it has tended to think in terms of bringing the whole of society under the church (or kingdom of God), but has then found that that can easily lead to grave compromise. The result has not infrequently been that the more "spiritual" have taken up a negative attitude again with a stress on the need to create a pure Christian culture, or commune, within the world's culture, and an unwillingness to see any good in things which are not specifically Christian. There is little doubt that, hidden in this reaction, there has often been the influence of pagan thought. Ever since the period of Gnostic influence in the first century there have been those who tended to denigrate the body and all merely human, this-worldly activity, because such an attitude seemed to be more spiritual. This teaching continues today, manifesting itself in different forms of what I shall call "Christian asceticism."

The Bible, to the surprise of many, has a more positive view of culture than the ascetic tradition allows, and parts of it seem to be written quite specifically to counterbalance the tendency of the superspiritual enthusiasts to ignore or play down the positive value of our natural and cultural life in God's eyes.

Definitions of culture

First, however, some definitions. When we say that someone is a very cultured person we mean that he is widely read and has a good understanding of the thinking, arts, and outlook of his own and other civilizations. When people write about culture, however, they usually define the word, not in that narrow sense, but in a very wide sense. In fact one of the major problems in discussing culture is that the meaning of the term is rarely quite clear. Most writers start by defining it in the widest possible sense and then use it in fact in a much narrower one. Emil Brunner defines it in effect as "all that people do beyond biological necessity" (in his *Christianity and Civilization*). Richard Niebuhr also, in his in many ways excellent book, *Christ and Culture*, defines it as follows: "Culture is the 'artificial environment' which man superimposes on the natural. It comprises language, habits, ideas, beliefs, customs, social organization, inherited artifacts, technical processes, and values." Niebuhr, however, then goes on to describe some Christians as "against culture," which would imply that they were against all language, habits, ideas, beliefs, customs, etc. In fact what he means is that they are against all secularized forms of culture and want to produce their own Christian culture. In most of his book he is talking about *culture* in the plural, not *culture*, singular and general. This is what I want to do here because, if culture is "all that people do beyond biological necessity," then the problem can be generalized thus: How do we do all this in a Christian way?

Today, however, and ever since the church began, the acute problems of culture have been how to react to the particular *cultures* in which the church finds itself. I want to define culture here in a sense that is between the narrow, popular sense and the very broad sense. For our purposes it may be described as "the overall beliefs, priorities, and values of the community that are expressed in its institutions and its practices (including of course its arts and architecture)." Tony Walter has described it as "lifestyle," and if we understand that in a very wide sense it might do as a brief definition, though I think its orientation is too practical and could ignore the fundamental outlooks which are part of culture. In the sense that I have given the term there can be a Marxist, Muslim, or Christianized culture. There can be a Western European culture or an urban or working-class culture. I believe the fundamental question is how we react to that kind of entity rather than how we react to culture in the widest sense.

Christian attitudes to culture

The most acute problem for the Christian arises because he finds himself in a culture that is a mixture of good and evil. Not only is it not thoroughly Christian, but it has some positively false emphases whose pervasive influence on the way we think and live tends to push us into false priorities and values. Not only that, but when the Christian tries to bring his culture more into conformity with Christian standards, he faces all sorts of difficult questions, from the problems of language (can he use pagan words for "God" to describe the living God?), through subtle questions of marriage and money, to problems about music and social life. Some of these things may have been formed in a non-Christian culture and now need to be either adopted by the church or replaced by something more fitting to a Christian community. Can certain forms of music, for instance, be used by the church to express a Christian outlook? Are a system of dowries or a period of engagement before marriage to be adopted, modified, or scrapped? Is beauty in buildings, home decoration, and clothes to be pursued if it involves greater expense? How important is it? Can capitalism or socialism be called "Christian," or do they need to be reformed or rejected? Are middle-class values simply good, bad, indifferent, or a mixture of Christian tradition with materialistic overtones? In almost every situation there are good and bad features. As one might expect in a community of fallen men and women, nothing is perfect. But equally, the world is not hell. There are in every culture things that the Christian ought to praise and reinforce.

It is helpful, I believe, to classify the three main attitudes to culture that have been important in the Christian church. I will do this first, trying to describe them in broad outlines, before going on to develop a positive view.[1]

1. The "love-not-the-world" emphasis

This school of thought is based upon such passages as 1 John 2:15–17, "Do not love the world or the things in the world"; 1 Corinthians 1–3; and 1 Peter 2:11. It emphasizes that we cannot serve God and mammon (Matt. 6:24) and "the whole world is in the power of the evil one" (1 John 5:19). From these and other Scriptures it concludes that the Christian should have as little as possible to do with the culture around him, but should create his own Christian culture within the world.

Positive involvement with non-Christians in all forms is frowned upon—except for the purposes of evangelism. The Christian life, its advocates stress, is to be lived out in a Christian community, or in a Christian church, in isolation from the rest. The monastic ideal of the medieval church illustrates this well. Public office, politics, or even business (except perhaps in a Christian firm) are in this view inappropriate for the spiritually minded Christian and lead only to his being "squeezed into the world's mold" (Rom. 12:2), or having to adopt "worldly ideas and methods." It is impossible to be a real friend of sinners (Jesus is an exception because he is sinless). The ideal is to deny the world in the widest possible sense of that word—that is to say, it is in principle an *ascetic* ideal. It has often led to vows of celibacy and poverty.

This negative attitude to culture (for brevity I will use the word "ascetic" because that is really what it is) is a streak in many Christian traditions. It has often been most strong in churches

---

[1] Richard Niebuhr classifies attitudes to culture under five headings, but I believe that this division into three main emphases is more helpful.

where the elders have less education than their children. Confronted with many new things and with their children going up the social scale and changing their lifestyle, they have often over-reacted. The children are then treated to constant warnings of the dangers of education, of money, of reading literature, of the arts and TV, etc. In the end it begins to sound like a largely negative attitude to almost all the good things of life. Even food and marriage and healthy social life begin to seem second best. Of course, the older generation may genuinely detect a creeping worldliness in their children; but they easily give the impression that the Christian cannot be positive about society, about the fruits of science, technology, or the arts, or about anything that is not specifically "Christian." "If in doubt, don't" is a maxim which is devastating in its effects if there is then doubt about almost everything except prayer, Bible study, and hymn singing. This situation can easily arise, so that any change of lifestyle is regarded as worldliness.

The extreme of this position is the hermit tradition. Here people withdrew from almost all social contact and tried to live purely "spiritual" lives stripped, as far as possible, of all social or even biological existence. In a moderate form it leads to many of the variety of Christian communes and communities where there is a refusal of art, music, social life, and education except insofar as these can be done in an explicitly Christian way. You may enjoy Christian songs, but not secular ones; Christian fellowship, but not friendship with non-Christians. Eve's temptation was a cultural one: the fruit "was good food, and . . . a delight to the eyes, and . . . to be desired to make one wise" (Gen. 3:6, which is probably the basis of 1 John 2:16). Therefore we must be constantly on our guard. The so-called radical Reformation tradition, of which the Anabaptists were leaders in the sixteenth century, followed this emphasis. Although radical in their view of the church, they were in this respect far from radical. They were, in fact, nearer to the monastic ideals of the unreformed church. Most Baptist churches today do not follow this ideal, but this school is exemplified in groups such as the Amish people—an extreme variety of the Mennonites who still, in the midst of modern American technology, do not (or did not until very recently) use razors, buttons, or automobiles. To call these people "against culture" is misleading; they are against secular cultures. They can be recognized immediately by their own unique culture—horses instead of cars, clasps instead of buttons, etc. The simple life—usually with a rural image—is seen as the Christian's ideal.

For many Evangelicals that outlook has a powerful appeal. They ask whether there is not something more spiritual in doing without the world's goods. If we are to love the world, must we not repudiate it? If the world's values are a threat, must we not avoid the world? To these people the cities seem a symbol of evil. To build office blocks for big business is somehow in itself a piece of worldliness. Technology and even scientific advance are seen more as a threat than a cause for any thankfulness to God. A recent book coming out of this tradition and described as "Essays on Christian Faith and Professionalism" has an almost entirely negative attitude and emphasis on the dangers of moving into the professional world. Many of the authors seem doubtful as to whether they ought to have moved from the rural environment. Significantly, the overall title of the book is *The Perils of Professionalism.*[2]

Ronald Sider, in his book *Rich Christians in an Age of Hunger,* has a considerable element of this tradition (he was a Mennonite). Thus he holds up as a model a science professor who has given up his job to live on clothes provided by the Salvation Army and "scavenging in vacant lots and junk piles, delighting to find some use from what other people discard," "foraging for supplies of berries, nuts, fruits and fireplace wood which otherwise would have gone to waste. Having a VW makes scrounging easier and shopping cheaper." This ideal of a simpler lifestyle certainly has its appeal; but it is frankly parasitic on those who do work to produce goods, and it is hard to see how it actually helps anyone in the poorer countries or in the community as a whole. Certainly the Third World would suffer severely if all Christians adopted this pattern and decided to

---

[2]Edited by Donald B. Kraybill and Phyllis Palmann Goode (Herald Press, 1982). The authors are all Mennonites.

abstain from coffee, tea, chocolate, quality cotton, and tropical fruits (personally, I have paused with thankfulness at this point to make myself a cup of tea. I have no sense that it would have been more godly to use cold water). More fundamentally, however, we need to ask if this model of the Christian attitude to culture is biblical and whether it resembles that of the early church (see below).

Now the Mennonites are to be admired, among other things, for their social work of relief and philanthropy. While some other people just talk, they get on with the job. No doubt also, the ex-professor whom Sider praises is a very fine and devoted Christian whose life may have important things to teach us. The question is, however, whether this is really a biblical ideal.

This emphasis has some important correctives for any tendency to materialism. We are commanded not to *love* the world. We must not value any of the gifts of our humanity and our culture as if they were for eternity. Even marriage is for this life only and must not be our idol. Cultural riches bring no one nearer to God, and they all too easily become a snare. The biblical passages concerned certainly emphasize these truths, and we must not forget them. In Scripture, however, this emphasis does not stand alone.

2. The "good creation" emphasis

The mainstream Reformers—Luther, Calvin, and the Anglicans—believed, however, that they had rediscovered in the Bible a major emphasis that must balance these other scriptural passages. First of all, Jesus prayed that his disciples would be kept from evil while "in the world" though "not of the world." Indeed he actually said explicitly, "I do not pray that thou shouldst take them out of the world, but that thou shouldst keep them from the evil one." I do not think there is any other example of something that Jesus or his disciples specifically say they did *not* pray for. The early Christians were not withdrawn into a Christian culture or series of communes. Something has gone wrong if we make a Christian community the ideal within a mixed society when the Bible does not do so. I am forced to conclude that the real justification for the Christian commune or ghetto concept of Christian community is that it is a defense mechanism in an evil world—not that it has any positive biblical support. If there are circumstances where it can be justified on the purely practical grounds that you cannot survive without it, they must be very rare. Indeed the early church was clearly distributed through different households where many of them were slaves and had even to be exhorted not to *neglect* meeting together. In the strict Reformed tradition, and in some other evangelical traditions, there has also been an emphasis on the exclusively Christian club or social organization, e.g., some of the student organizations in countries such as Holland. The result of these has never been quite what was hoped. They have nearly always gone sour, developing a kind of private language and humor that nobody else can appreciate and giving a training that makes it even harder for Christians to live in the world afterwards. Again one must ask, is it a biblical pattern?

There are, however, other positive biblical corrections of the whole ascetic ideal. First Timothy seems to have been written partly to correct this "super spirituality." It contains an emphasis on the importance of good government (2:1–3), good physical health (5:23), and concern for the physical well-being of members of the family (5:3–8). Note that people who neglect this are "worse than an unbeliever." In 4:1–4 there is a resounding criticism of those who hold a negative attitude to food and marriage; Paul says they are perpetrating a "doctrine of demons." While he warns of the dangers of loving money, he also in the same chapter tells the rich to share their resources because God has given us richly all things to *enjoy* (6:10, 17–18). Pagan religions are often ascetic, and this is probably what Paul has in mind in his phrase about a "doctrine of demons" in 4:1. Christians must not imitate this often attractive feature of paganism. This is a lesson that the church failed to learn when it allowed Gnosticism to become influential and to create a long-term preference for the negative attitude to the body as in some way more spiritual.[3]

---

[3] Hindu leaders, such as Gandhi, often stress the virtues of self-denial as a

First Timothy is far from standing alone. Jesus himself in the Sermon on the Mount stresses that God cares for the material well-being of all men and that we are to do the same (Matt. 5:43–48). Jesus healed ten lepers even though only one said thank you. Other passages recommend marriage as the normal, but not universal, God-given pattern and encourage us to enjoy all God's material and social blessings. As 1 Timothy 4:4 puts it, "everything created by God is good," even in a fallen world. The examples Paul gives there of food and marriage should be taken as examples of God's gifts of natural resource on the one hand and of human capacity on the other. In that case, we are called to a positive and not a negative attitude to all the good things of culture, whether they are a safe water supply and good education, or art and music. All of these are at least capable of being part of the "everything created by God" which we are to "receive with thanksgiving," most especially if we "believe and know the truth." The Christian on this view ought to be more positive about the good gifts of culture than the non-Christian and more enthusiastic for the development of all its created possibilities. Far from being ascetic (i.e., believing it to be a virtue to go without) he will be wanting to ensure that all men *share* the resources as fully as possible and in wholesome ways. This, of course, may involve going without for the sake of supplying others, or for the sake of even more important gifts, but it would mean refusing to go without for its own sake. As Paul says in Colossians 2:23, that kind of self-denial, although it *appears* to be a virtue, does not in fact lead to spiritual progress.

There may be some positive reasons for self-denial. Paul himself seems to have gone without marriage (or possibly remarriage as a widower) and many other things that he had a right to ask for, for the sake of the ministry that God had given

---

means of spiritual progress—as in his autobiography. To him and to some Christians it is almost self-evident that it is more spiritual to be without sex, animal products for food, academic education, etc. They see these things as hindrances to spiritual maturity. The Bible does not, and it denounces this error in Colossians 2 and 1 Timothy 4. See *M. K. Gandhi: An Autobiography* (Penguin, 1982).

him (1 Cor. 9:1–12). A positive attitude to God's gifts certainly does not mean that we regard them all as *rights* to which we should lay claim. It does mean that we receive with thankfulness what we are given and regard the enrichment of our culture and our society as a positive Christian program. No one can have everything, and no one can develop every one of the gifts or potentialities that he has. But we must not regard it as better to be deprived or to leave our capacities undeveloped. Indeed they give us a social responsibility to do as well as we possibly can with the gifts that we have and which not so many other people may possess to the same degree.

A further qualification must be made, however. The good gifts can become too precious to us so that, in loving them, we make them an idol competing with God himself for our real motivation. These gifts are given to us in a fallen world where nothing is untouched by evil. This is peculiarly true of those aspects of culture that are the fruits of human intellectual or emotional activity. The emotions, the will, and the mind of man are all sinful, and men, especially but not exclusively those who have not known God's transforming grace, are bound to allow their sinfulness to taint the good gifts that they develop. As is evident to our friends, even if not to ourselves, we are not yet made perfect. Our art, architecture, or philosophy, therefore, are not going to be perfect. Cities have evil aspects, but so does rural life.

All culture is, then, a mixture of good and evil—good because God's gifts of creation are good, man is still in the image of God, and no man is a devil; but evil because no man is an angel. No one is perfect in this life. The structures of society and even the best aspects of our culture are therefore imperfect, and some of them are in themselves a recognition of the fallenness of the world, e.g., police forces, criminal lawyers, and many social and medical services. Sin taints all, and sin suddenly emerges in unexpected places. The best art and poetry is often marked by human conceit. Science and philosophy can be turned to evil uses. The university and even the hospital can present themselves not as a humble and grateful resource, passing on the benefits of God's creation, but as proud and self-important monuments to human cleverness.

The "good-creation" emphasis does not mean that culture is accepted without qualification. In fact it should result in emphasis on the need to try to *improve* it and to bring it increasingly into conformity with the will of God. Because this school believes that God *cares* for the health and this-worldly well-being of all men as well as for their eternal well-being, it teaches that *we must care*. It has resulted in a positive enthusiasm for cultural involvement guided by the principles of the Scriptures. Note that in 1 Timothy 4:4 these things are to be subject to "the word of God and prayer." This tradition has therefore been enthusiastic for enjoying art, music, architecture, good government, etc. and making all these human creations conform as nearly as possible to God's creation and providential ideals as revealed to us.

In practice the Ten Commandments form an extremely useful set of guidelines for our ideals in this area. Their implications need to be worked out, and Scripture often does this for us. But as practical guidelines the Commandments are much more fundamental and far-reaching than people often realize. Paul, in Ephesians 4:25–6:9 for instance, builds a whole picture of the Christian life on the structure of the Ten Commandments. He does so in a way that has close parallels with the Sermon on the Mount and obviously echoes our Lord's teaching there. When the Reformers set out the ideals of the Christian life around the Ten Commandments they were following an apostolic pattern and refusing to go along with the superspiritual emphasis that rejected the law as no longer relevant. Once more the Bible's guidelines are more practical and down to earth than some sophisticated writers about culture.

3. The liberal tradition: Christ "fulfilling culture"

At the other extreme to the "love-not-the-world" emphasis is the liberal tradition that sees Christianity as a fulfillment of man's own inbuilt ideals. This view cannot seriously claim any biblical support, though attempts in that direction have been made. As

Niebuhr describes it: "Jesus Christ is approached and understood as a great leader, the spiritual, cultural cause of man's struggle to subdue nature, and of his aspirations to transcend it." In this way it joins force with the love-not-the-world emphasis, and some social movements are a mixture of "overcoming nature" and "love-not-the-world" asceticism. Both fail to have a sufficiently positive view of the good gifts of God in creation. The Christian on this liberal view is called upon to learn from the world—or from Marxism, humanism, psychology, or any other cultural "insight" of mankind. Great poetry or drama or philosophy is expected to teach us what we need to know, though Jesus Christ is the apex and fulfillment of man's cultural ideals if only man can see it. Good music is thought to be spiritual, and no distinction of principle is made between aesthetic and spiritual experience. The aim of the church on this view is to create a true humanity. At a conference of leaders of this tradition the participants were recently asked to confess to God their "failure to be fully human." Of course the Bible teaches that full humanity is to be found in Christ; but the Bible tells us to repent of sin—rebellion against God—not of immaturity. Because this view does not see the radical difference between gifts for our human life on earth (which should lead us to thankfulness and repentance, Rom. 2:4) and God's supernatural gifts of grace, it ends up with an inadequate appreciation of both.

How do we choose?

If these three options describe the main Christian views in outline, how do we choose between them? First, let it be said that each has something true about it. The liberal tradition makes us look at the real world and warns us that our theological themes can be doctrinaire and can be too much a defense of our own interests without sufficient regard to how they actually work out in practice. That is not an unbiblical stress. Our Lord said, "By their fruits you shall know them." The two other traditions each contain an important biblical emphasis which has to be grasped if we are to be biblical Christians. Insofar as these views have polarized, there has been a danger of minimizing the valid emphasis of the other views.

Second, it is important to state that if you lean decisively to one or another view, that does not mean you have to go along with the rest of the system of theology with which it is normally associated. You do not, for instance, have to be a systematic Calvinist in the old tradition to believe that, in this particular area of thought, this tradition has got it right, and has the best track record historically. Equally, you do not have to be radical in your doctrine of the church if you are inclined to accept the Mennonite tradition about culture.

Third, all of these traditions have often suffered historically from a progressive dilution of their real Christian inspiration. Secularization has set in all too easily, and the ascetic approach has become an escape from human responsibility to a parasitic kind of monasticism (not all monasticism was escapist, especially at its beginning). A creation ordinance approach has been turned into an excuse for uncontrolled profit making and for liberty from moral restraints and from concern for people. We must not, however, blame any tradition for its secularized version. We can learn from these historical skeletons that each is vulnerable in particular ways to serious abuses against which we must guard ourselves. We must judge each by its most self-consistent expression.

I want to argue that the middle option (God's good creation tradition) is the only one that is solidly biblical, and, if it will also listen to what the others have to say that is biblical, it is the most convincing way of approaching the problem. I believe it also has a far better historical record behind it than the other traditions. I do not believe that the others can in the same way take in the positive emphases of the alternatives, and there are serious weaknesses in the resulting outlook to which they lead.

Toward a constructive Christian view

Starting with the particular passages mentioned in 1 Timothy, we must accept that the New Testament has a positive estimate of the material world, of the good things of life, of bodily health,

THE INTELLECT AND BEYOND

and of the state as an ordinance of God's providence. Jesus healed bodies and minds and cared for the whole man when he "had compassion on them." There is no trace in Jesus' own teaching of a negative attitude to the body, except when he is in fact saying that other, eternal things are much *more* important. He taught that God's care for all men sends the sun and the rain even for the wicked, and that we are to care like that for the material this-worldly needs of all men. The disciples were sent out not only to preach the gospel, but also to heal and to cast out demons. We are to pray for good government (1 Tim. 2:1–6) and to see it as a gift of God's providence (Rom. 13:1–8; 1 Peter 2:13–17) so that we cooperate with it in all that is good.

Second, 1 Timothy 4:1–10 includes among other good things the created *capacities of men* for marriage and the *natural resources* of food. The passage then generalizes them by saying, "For [i.e., the reason for this positive attitude is] *everything* created by God is good, and nothing is to be rejected if it is received with thanksgiving." This passage, with 1 Timothy 6:17–19, where we are told that God has given us richly all things to enjoy (the context is what money can buy), and other New Testament passages, combine to give us the picture of an essentially positive Christian attitude to government, to health, to good food, to marriage and family life—indeed to social and cultural life generally. The Old Testament undoubtedly confirms this when material prosperity and rich family life are frequently seen as God's blessings, and poverty and loneliness as deprivations which we should exert ourselves to overcome.

What then of the apparently negative attitude of 1 John 2:15–17, et al.? Why does Jesus say in Luke 14:26, "If anyone comes to me and does not hate his own father and mother and wife and children and brothers and sister, yes, and even his own life, he cannot be my disciple," if in other passages of the Bible we are urged to care for our parents and other dependent relatives (Mark 7:9–13; 1 Tim. 5:3–8)? The best short answer, to take only one example, is to point out that even in 1 Timothy 6, where Paul goes on in verse 17 to say that the rich should share their *good* things because "He richly furnishes us with everything to enjoy," he precedes that section by a warning against loving money and against caring for unneeded comfort and luxury: "But those who desire to be rich fall into temptation, into a snare, into many senseless and hurtful desires that plunge men into ruin and destruction. For the love of money is the root of all evils." We cannot possibly try to oppose the teaching of John to Paul, as some, including Niebuhr, have tried to do. Paul has the same warnings and deliberately puts them side by side with his positive emphasis in the same chapter. He demonstrated his attitude in his own rugged life. He gloried in his deprivations *for the sake of* the gospel. The phrase, "for his sake I have suffered the loss of all things, and count them as refuse, in order that I may gain Christ and be found in him," is Paul, not John. There cannot be an opposition between this positive view of material things and the view that they are not the Christian's priority. The Christian, therefore, must not be trapped into *loving* them (using the word "love" in a very strong sense), but he should admire and be thankful for all that is good, because it is the fruit of God's creation and providence.

We must, therefore, hold these two things together. While we care for people's this-worldly health, comfort, and well-being, we must remember that there are more important things in life. If we have to choose, then spiritual things come first. Paul, however, stresses that this does not mean neglect of our health, our family, or our reading and study. We do not normally have to choose. We are to pursue both health of body and health of spirit, both social well-being and moral well-being, as any parent knows who cares for his own children. The emphasis in Paul and John and above all in the teaching of Jesus makes plain that, partly just because these material and cultural things are good and attractive to us, they can be a danger. "To the pure all things are pure," says Paul. But we all know that it is very difficult to be rich and pure, or to be very gifted culturally and not to make our gifts into an idol.

Eve's temptation was not that the tree was good for food, beautiful, and wisdom-giving. Its beauty was God-given in a perfect world and was to be admired. The Devil persuaded her to make these genuinely and rightly attractive features more important than God's will and explicit command. This must not lead us to despise beauty. It must warn us that God-given beauty can become too important to us.

There is no conflict in these two biblical emphases. Whereas the "God's good creation" emphasis can take in the warnings of Scripture, an opposite emphasis which makes 1 John 2 and similar passages its main starting point, finds it impossible in practice fully to accept the positive emphasis of the Bible on the limited, but God-given, value of culture. There always remains a niggling desire to do without for its own sake and to find fault with cultural activities so as to exalt by contrast a more "spiritual" concept. The result is that the ascetic tradition has produced very few people who have advanced knowledge in science or technology or have been willing to get involved in business or government. Indeed, some of them have argued explicitly that these things should be left to the unconverted. Those who stress the "God's good creation" tradition need to be shaken up by the more ascetic tradition. It presents a challenge to those who are in danger of getting caught up with materialism and "the love of money." Even in the Old Testament the Nazirites who took an ascetic vow were intended as a protest and a reminder of the danger of materialism and reliance on things. We can admire with thankfulness those who today live out such an ideal and be thankful that they reprove our love of ease and selfish comforts. But, as in the Old Testament, the Nazirites were not intended to be the idol. Even Jesus himself was criticized for his lack of asceticism. He enjoyed food and drink and social life. He was therefore called "a glutton and a drunkard" (Matt. 11:19) by those who believed that a really spiritual man must have a negative attitude in such matters.

A dangerous ideal

Indeed, the example of Jesus expresses it perfectly. He was incarnate in a very imperfect culture. He lived under Roman law and told his disciples to pay taxes to the imperialist conquerors. He attended weddings and dinners in the homes of unbelievers. He was a friend of sinners. He spoke their imperfect language, lived according to their imperfect customs, and in this he contrasted with the ascetic John the Baptist. And even if John the Baptist is an easier character to identify with, Jesus, and not John, is our ideal. The ascetic tradition is nearer to John the Baptist, but, as Jesus stressed, John was the last of the prophets. "He that is least in the kingdom of heaven is greater than he" (Matt. 11:11). The new Christian order has a new, more positive approach—partly just because the Holy Spirit is given to all believers to enable them to live by such a dangerous ideal.

The ascetic tradition seems safer in a fallen world. But it is oversafe and cannot in fact achieve the New Testament ideals. Like the ascetic series of negative rules described in Colossians 2, it sounds good and impressive but does not achieve what is meant to be achieved another way. We must seek to live as New Testament Christians *in the world*, in the power of the Holy Spirit, and to make our culture approximate as nearly as we can to the biblical ideal insofar as we have any opportunity of altering it.

Christians in all traditions—and not least Evangelicals— have found this balance hard to maintain. All too easily the spiritually minded have slipped into a hidden or open asceticism. This focuses sometimes in denying to the rising generation cultural activities that they have good reasons for valuing. Their music, social life, and education need constant criticism by the Word of God, but the older generation often give the impression that it would be more godly to live an exclusively religious life in a way that makes nonsense to the young, to those in education, or to those with a young family. On the other side, we are all in danger of creeping materialism. Here the young are often critical of the members of the older generation who, they feel, are too materialistic. The old are felt to have forgotten to apply strict moral criteria to their professions and to the priorities of a Christian mind in their lifestyle. This conflict is not really in the least about generations, of course, but it is easier for the young with few commitments to live loose to possessions, and it is easier for the old to live loose to cultural riches of other kinds. We need to listen to one another, but above all to the Bible, which insists that we value God's creation and providential gifts and, at the same time, keep our priorities right so that we are glad to go without good things when it is necessary for the sake of "the kingdom of God and his righteousness," which we are to seek *first.*

The relative autonomy of human institutions

The "God's good creation" emphasis is also not at all incompatible with believing that human study and knowledge and institutions should have a *relative* autonomy. It is quite incompatible with the idea that anything in the world can be autonomous of the lordship of Christ and his revealed truth. But music, for instance, may be judged good music when it has no clear theological emphasis. Parents must make decisions for their children where the church has no concern.

The point is most clearly illustrated in the New Testament attitude to the not-at-all Christian state authority of the day, and in the Old Testament attitude to non-Jewish authorities such as Egypt and Babylon. We have several passages in the teachings of Christ, Paul, and Peter dealing with this topic. We also have examples of what the teaching meant in practice in the Acts. The state is seen as an ordinance of God's providential and creation order. We imagine that even in a sinlessly perfect world someone would have to decide on which side of the road you drive your carriage or car. In the New Testament we are talking about pagan powers in a mixed society in which the Christians also are far from perfect. There is no encouragement for Christians to be other than helpful members of the imperfect community. Our Lord's phrase "render therefore to Caesar the things that are Caesar's and to God the things that are God's," firmly taught that we have a distinct and positive duty to a secular, in many ways evil, ruling power. At the same time, it puts alongside that our superior duty to God. The early Christians in Acts, therefore, obeyed the "powers" except where the powers tried to compel them to do what conflicted with their duty to God. They were positive about the powers (see, e.g., Acts 16:35–40) but made it plain, exactly as Jesus had done, that the relative autonomy of the state was not a complete autonomy. Moral and theological issues come first. Nevertheless the state may fix its own level of taxation and we are to pay cheerfully, even if we do not approve everything that is done with the money (Rom. 13:6).

The state, therefore, has, under God, a relatively autonomous area of life for which there are distinctive instructions in Scripture. The attempt by some in the ascetic tradition to identify the "principalities and powers" in Ephesians 6 and other passages with governments and other cultural institutions is an impossible exposition of a passage which is talking about personal temptation. Whereas the state in the Book of Revelation can emerge as an embodiment of the Devil when it persecutes the church, the Bible has in both Old Testament and New Testament an essentially positive view of the role of the state as an ordinance of God. The explicit teaching on the subject in the Bible should help us to see other cultural institutions similarly. They are not totally bad or totally good. They can become an agent of evil, but they remain better than anarchy and must be persuaded to function in accordance with the will and law of God. They are, however, not the church. Some of the instructions for the church are not relevant for the state, while other (and not lower) standards may be given, as in Romans 13, for the state.

Outline of a Christian view

Let me, then, try to clarify some outlines of a Christian view of culture that may help us toward a practical policy.

1. Through both Creation and Providence, God has given us artistic and cultural gifts to enable us to bring into being a rich and varied culture for our this-worldly benefit. These gifts, like rain, are for all people—Christians and non-Christians, good and bad alike—without any evident distinction. They are part of the creation mandate to "subdue the earth" (Gen. 1:28).

2. The culture so created is a benefit. Even a very imperfect state is better than anarchy. Wholesome family life can be enjoyed by non-Christians and Christians alike and is part of God's wish for all people. Lifelong marriage, parental instincts for the care of children, and delight in their responsive love are

things for which God cares. Beauty—our enjoyment of nature, art, and music—is something which we are to enjoy and find of human benefit. All these things minister to (or are intended to be so well-structured as to minister to) our health and well-being and a rich use of God's world. They do not in themselves lead us nearer to God, but they are a great blessing for this life. They are good in themselves and therefore humanly helpful. Paul advised Titus: "Insist . . . that those who have believed in God may be careful to apply themselves to good deeds [or honest occupations]; these are excellent and profitable to men" (Tit. 3:8). Such things should lead us to thankfulness and to repentance.

3. This is so, even though in a fallen world nothing is perfect. We find evil in our own hearts even at the points of highest human bliss. The most splendid human artifacts are not free from the touch of human sin. We must not, therefore, polarize things so that all cultural products are seen either as Christian or humanistic. All are, in fact, a mixture of what is pleasing to God and what is not. They are judged relatively "good" or "bad" art, architecture, family life, etc., according to their degree of conformity to their proper (God-given) function.

4. All cultural gifts are for this life only. In themselves they are not of eternal value, though how we use them may be of eternal significance. Good music is not in itself spiritual, though it may be used to convey spiritual truth effectively. We cannot despise cultural excellence, since we see it as a gift from God; but we cannot make it the main thing in life. A Christian mind will always cut it down to size in a way that may make us ridiculous in the eyes of our professional contemporaries who live for it. I recently heard a university professor say, "We must first learn to despise culture and scholarship—to 'consider them rubbish' (Phil. 3:8)—before we can give them their positive Christian value."

5. For these and other reasons, we are to be kept from the idolatry of culture or even from the idolatry of trying to make a perfect culture. It cannot be done. Ever since Babel, attempts have been made. Even so-called Christian cultures or Christian arts or Christian poetry are full of reflections of fallen human nature. Indeed, calling a cultural unit "Christian," whether it is

a school, a poem, or a family, has the grave danger that we pretend it is perfect when we know it is not.

Furthermore, we can never idolize our nation or our political stance. Nehemiah wept for the sins of his nation even while he sought to restore its fortunes. Pride of nationality was often condemned in the Old Testament even while the writers gave thanks for all that was good in the nation. Politics, nationality, art, and education must all be seen both as temporary and imperfect features of this life only and yet as important aspects of our Christian responsibility.

6. We cannot opt out of the world. What we can do is to live our cultural life as fully as possible under the lordship of Christ. That will mean living in the world with a heart and mind and will renewed and controlled as far as we are aware by God's revelation. These things are to be controlled, as 1 Timothy 4:4 says, "by the word of God and prayer." The Bible gives us our priorities and our guidelines for life in a non-Christian culture.

7. Meanwhile we shall appreciate and value whatever is good in the culture in which we are set, by the standards of God's revelation, even if those things that are good do not at all derive from a Christian understanding of the world. There will be things "true, honorable, just, pure, lovely, gracious and worthy of praise" (Phil. 4:8) in the most anti-Christian of societies. People in communist countries are right to try to be good citizens, to strengthen all that is good, and to praise what those societies may have achieved in honesty, mutual concern, justice, etc. We are to cooperate even with a wicked Caesar.

8. We should also seek the good of our culture. It is not moral and spiritual compromise to work for better education in a state school or in a humanistic society or for integrity in business or in our profession. We need not and should not retreat into an exclusively Christian business, trade association, or community life. If we do, we shall find that it is only relatively more Christian, and that evil is still in our own natures and in the structure of this supposedly Christian subculture. Even after a reformation (or a revolution) there will still be evil in the structure of the society and in our own hearts.

9. We must be modest about our Christian contribution.

Our primary concern is with eternal life. Thus, while bodily exercise is of some value for the Christian, godliness is of value both for this life and for the life to come (1 Tim. 4:8). Our main contribution *as Christians* is in the latter area. Since, however, we are to love the whole man, we care about both. So we shall be enthusiastic to do whatever we can for the enrichment of culture at a purely creation–providential level. If we can reduce poverty, improve health, and build beautiful and economical and socially healthy buildings, we shall be delighted. We shall know, however, that these things in themselves get no one nearer to heaven, and therefore we cannot make them our main ambition in life. Neither can we claim that Christian contributions to culture have always been an unqualified success. The Christian is not automatically better at these things than others, and it is easy for Christians to make major mistakes through being overconfident and lacking the relevant wisdom.

10. Within culture there may be areas of relative autonomy. The Christian may need, as we say, to wear a different hat in different circumstances—as a church member, as a parent, or as a marriage partner. Responsibilities may at times seem to conflict. As an official of the state, he may be called upon to exercise the sort of ministry that he ought never to exercise in the church. For instance, he may be a minister of God's wrath (Rom. 13:4). This is one reason that the judge or policeman often wears a distinctive uniform—to identify the role in which he is now active. Paul is careful to place side by side the Christian ideal for individual relationships (see Rom. 12:14–21, where he almost exactly quotes the Sermon on the Mount) and the fact that God has appointed certain people to exercise vengeance on evil (see Rom. 13:1–5). Thus, things that we ought not to do in our personal capacity as Christians we might have to do in our public capacity as servants of the state. Although the chapter division has obscured the fact, it is no accident that these two things stand side by side.

The state has its own God-given standards, which in some important ways differ from those of personal Christian relationships. Science, art, and family life have some rules, criteria, and methods that are different from those in other spheres. For example, parents may, and sometimes should, punish their own children, not (in the same way) their neighbor's children; and the style of punishment may differ in different spheres.

11. The Ten Commandments, because they give us a very practical outline of our ideals, are to be our rule for a mixed society. This point needs further justification, for which there is no space here. This means, however, that for us, *personal morality comes first.* Someone who promotes some great new idea in architecture or business and yet is dishonest in work or neglects marriage vows is not thinking or acting Christianly.

12. In the Protestant tradition we probably now need to be most careful that we do not misuse the positive emphasis on culture and the belief in the relative autonomy of particular spheres to allow us to become frankly secular or materialistic. If the gifts of culture are good, and they are, then we are most tempted to let the pursuit of these good things justify wrong means or a failure to be as careful about our motives as we should. We cannot say "business is business" if that means allowing dishonesty or the abuse of our power. We can aspire to do a better job than anyone else is doing in the service of the community. We can aspire to build up a business that pays good wages and produces a good economical and useful product, but not if it means living for success or money. Similarly, we can aspire to expand our department in a school, if we are satisfied that it will be good for the pupils and for society. But our "empire building" must not denigrate the good that others are doing or hope to do. We must see our role in a Christian perspective of the whole activity. The positive emphasis here can be misused—when evil is justified by calling it by some other name; but we must not shrink back for that reason. A negative emphasis has in the long run created even greater damage.

13. Nevertheless, this does not mean that God's revealed will gives us a blueprint for culture. The analogy of nature warns us that this could be very dangerous. The quite incredible variety of birds, flowers, animals, etc., none of which can be said to be the ideal as opposed to any other, indicates that God delights in variety. He has, as it were, so many different ways of doing the same thing, and this is partly the cause of our own

delight in nature. Similarly, variety in cultural tradition can be a great enrichment, and we must not suggest that there is a particular kind of music, painting, architecture, or furniture that is in a unique sense Christian, any more than there is a particular flower that is more God-honoring than others. All must be under the rule of Christ. But that still leaves enormous responsibility for us in our own society. For our own and other people's enjoyment and, in the broadest sense, health, we must create that which will minister to their this-worldly good. Indeed, the Christian ideal of health in body, mind, and spirit provides a good way of thinking about our cultural role in education, art, architecture, science, medicine, etc. We are interested that people should be truly healthy.

14. The Christian should therefore value creative freedom in culture—knowing that "this service is perfect freedom." Freedom is only freedom if it operates within the structures of reality (i.e., creation). Destructive vandals are not expressing freedom; rather, they are showing their bondage to irrational and uncontrolled impulses. Freedom is part of God's purpose for his people (Gal. 5:1). Jesus came that we might have life and might have it more abundantly (John 10:10). Freedom, innovation, and enterprise are in themselves part of God's creation purpose. But they are not certificates for moral license (Gal. 5:13). True freedom and initiative are found only under the authority of God's Word and prayer, because our God is also our Creator, and he has instructed us to live in a way that is exactly suited to our real needs and our real nature. With this confidence, the Christian should not be merely safe and mediocre in his cultural activities; instead, he should enjoy a freedom such as nobody else enjoys and a positive vision for the cultural task that nobody else can share. Just because it is not his idol *to be served*, he can with joy and thankfulness to God make it *to be a servant* of the glory of God and the life we are given to lead here on earth.

9

Developing a Christian mind

How then can we grow a Christian mind? How can we obey the command to be continuously renewed in the spirit of our minds? How in fact can we arrive at a position of loving God with all our minds?

If what I have written so far is even broadly correct, a Christian mind should be thought of as a Christian outlook (or perhaps better "onlook") on life. Because it is based on God's revealed truth it enables us to think and therefore to live in accordance with his will. The apostle John can speak of the Christian life as *"following the truth"* (2 John 4). In that case the answer to those questions about how to develop a Christian mind will be something along the following lines.

1. What God wants of us first of all is our unreserved and wholehearted love, a love that employs all our powers. That must include our thinking. Without that element our discipleship is very seriously defective, and our daily lives will be displeasing to him and far less of a credit to our Lord than they should and could be. We must remember, however, that the Lord does not want our minds alone. He wants equally the love of our heart, soul, and strength. It is possible to be unbalanced in our stress on the mind, and, even if the present age leans the other way and the chief danger is to be mindless in our Christian

service, we never help in the long run by being unbalanced in any direction from a biblical point of view.

I was once at an important meeting in which a well-known Christian made the remark, "Since the whole evangelical world is erring by leaning in one direction, we can afford to be unbalanced in the other." I was thankful to somebody else in the group who then said, "Before we lean to the right hand or to the left, I want to know what is the perpendicular so that we may keep to that." In the past the Christian church has paid a terrible price for being unbalanced even when it was an effort to correct the balance of somebody else. Frankly, to be unbalanced means to be unbiblical. We must keep to the perpendicular.

2. Our mind is controlled by what we know is true. It must be granted that no one is altogether consistent here. We do not always allow the truth to rule us. We are good at finding reasons for whatever we want to believe and do. Jesus said to his opponents in John 5:44, "How can you believe, who receive glory from one another and do not seek the glory that comes from the only God?" To those whose fundamental desires were wrong it became impossible to believe what was staring them in the face. Our minds are easily captured by our affections rather than, as they are meant to be, by truth. The Christian, however, is freed to see and believe the truth, and the biblical command is to follow that truth both in evangelism (we preach Christ and him crucified so that men may respond to the truth) and in the Christian's progress. Having a new nature we can now function as we are made to function. We must therefore allow truth to rule us. If, for instance, we believe that God is faithful to his promises, then we are able to set aside the prospect of immediate short-term gains for the hope that is before us. Our affections can and should be ruled by truth. It is said even of Jesus that "for the joy that was set before him [He] endured the cross, despising the shame, and is seated at the right hand of the throne of God" (Heb. 12:2). What we need as well as a heart renewed by the Holy Spirit is a mind renewed by the Holy Spirit in its living grasp of truth, so that our affections and our minds work together to rule us in the Christian life.

But what we believe is meant to control what we know we ought to do. In the history of God's people this has been obviously so. Christianity was created by truth; above all by Christ who embodies truth. False doctrine has repeatedly led to un-Christian living, just as the New Testament says it would. Christianity is not just better sense arrived at by growth in human knowledge. It is the result of God's having *spoken*, above all in his Son, and of men who believed the Word and acted on it.

3. There is a difference in the way God works in our hearts and in our minds. Becoming a personal Christian is often described in the Bible in terms of Christ himself, or the Holy Spirit, entering a person's life or "heart" (see, e.g., Eph. 3:17; Rev. 3:20). The result is what is described in John 3 as a "new birth." Totally new desires are created, and we find that our affections have been radically redirected. When we are born again our minds are recentered on God, but they are not totally reordered at a stroke. We find our minds progressively reordered as we take on board an increasing appreciation of what is the truth and the will of God. Thus Paul in Romans 12:2 can talk to people who have been Christians for some time, telling them to be continuously transformed by the renewal of their minds.

This is not to suggest that the heart is suddenly made perfect and the mind unaltered by becoming a Christian. As we have said, being a Christian in itself involves having seen the truth and having our whole outlook on life started in a new direction. The Christian is often acutely aware of a tug of war between old and new affections, but he is "a new creation." There is a new direction to life and a new power. This cannot come about without a change of mind also. That is the meaning of repentance. Our minds are opened to know and believe the truth, and by God's grace we turn to follow it. Once we are Christians, however, growth in the Christian life comes very largely by growth of knowledge (in the mind), followed by obedience (in the will), because we have been made to love what God loves and hate what he hates. In the New Testament, this is nearly always stressed as a progressive thing, one great aspect of growing in Christian maturity (or sanctification), whereas the new birth is a one-time work of God in the soul (or heart).

The "hinge" section of Colossians expresses this concisely. In Colossians 3, after telling us in verses 1 and 2 to "seek [NIV, "set your *hearts* on"] the things that are above and then "Set your *minds* on things that are above," Paul continues in verses 9 and 10, "You have put off the old nature with its practices and have put on the new nature, which is being renewed in knowledge after the image of its creator." You have a new nature (new birth), he says, and you are to experience renewal in knowledge. At first sight the idea that being "renewed after the image of its creator" should be in the area of "knowledge" is surprising, but this is completely in accordance with Paul's repeated prayer for Christians that they grow in knowledge, that they know the truth needed for right action, etc. When the mind grasps truth in a fresh way we are able to make progress in Christlikeness. Without being renewed in knowledge of the real state of affairs in God's world—the truth—we cannot grow. Remember that ignorance is one of the marks of the non-Christian (Eph. 4:18). One great feature of the image of God is here described as knowledge—our eyes are opened so that we know the truth. That is the beginning of our transformation. Also, incidentally, as in Ephesians 4:23, the verb *being renewed* is a present continuous tense implying an ongoing process even though we are said already to have put off the old and to have put on the new nature. We make continuous progress in knowledge so that we may live out what we are, by virtue of having a new nature. This statement in Colossians 3 leads on to the marvelous exhortation to holiness in our relationships and then to verses 14–16: "Above all these put on love. Let the peace of Christ rule in your hearts. . . . Let the word of Christ dwell in you richly, [as you] teach and admonish one another in all wisdom. It is once more this biblical balance or, rather, a dual and equal stress on the heart and the mind as the means of growth and stability in a Christian life.

Let me illustrate this. A student from a non-Christian background was converted to faith in Christ without having an opportunity study the Bible much or to fill his mind with

Christian teaching. About six weeks after he had become a Christian, he was reading the Bible with a Christian friend. When they came to a particular passage about sexual immorality he suddenly said, "Does that mean I ought to stop sleeping with my girl friend? I had never thought of that." Now you might expect that a great internal tussle began as he tried to justify what he found forbidden. In fact it was for him a fairly simple matter, because his heart was changed by the new birth. When he had made quite sure that the Bible did insist on it, he was fully prepared to obey. His new birth had not automatically warned him that this was not part of the "good and acceptable and perfect" will of God. When his mind was instructed in it, however, he was now able to do what he would not have done before and to do so believing that God had something better. I have seen the same sort of progress in someone who at first did not see anything wrong in being drunk every Saturday night, as he had been before he became a Christian. There can be a struggle of course, and Jesus warns us of it. He said that the cares of the world and the delight in riches choke the Word for some and that they never grow up as Christians or become fruitful. Therefore Paul prayed constantly for his converts that they might *grow* in knowledge and in understanding. For instance, in Colossians 1, after having given thanks for their genuine faith, love, and hope, he says, "And so, from the day we heard of it, we have not ceased to pray for you, asking that you may be filled with the *knowledge* of his will in all spiritual *wisdom* and *understanding*, to lead a life worthy of the Lord, fully pleasing to him, bearing fruit in every good work and increasing in the *knowledge* of God." We need to know and understand the truth better if we are to live better.

4. We are, then, to be ruled by God's *Word* and *Spirit*. The Spirit gives us new life (but it is also said that we are born again by the Word of God) and the Word (which was written by the Spirit of God through his servants) rules our minds, our hope, our faith, and so in turn our affections. We must not separate the Word and the Spirit any more than we separate the heart and the mind of man. We do not, therefore, just indulge in

academic study of the Bible; that can be very dry. But the Bible is given to us to mold our life through our thinking. It comes to us through the mind as we seek to understand it in the right way. Thus in 1 Corinthians 15, Paul insists that only a right belief about our resurrection can prevent wrong attitudes to life and give us the right attitude to both life and death. A wrong doctrine of resurrection undermines morality and leads us to say, "Let us eat and drink, for tomorrow we die." The *Bible's method*—from truth to life—must be our pattern.

5. In practice this means that we must fill our minds with the revealed truth of God that he has given us in the Bible. It is not just a control by Bible verses. As we have stressed, the Bible makes it much wider than that; spiritual growth comes through "the word of God and prayer." It is the spirit of our minds that has to be changed so that we may grasp spiritual truth in a right way. We are given, however, a pattern of truth and Christian life, and not merely a set of unrelated truths or rules. It works from truth revealed to a life which is not merely correct, but is molded by the Spirit of God through his written Word.

6. We are to learn (with the Bible's method and agenda before us) to apply the truths to our life. I have tried to give some biblical examples of this method and some modern examples. It is a process which is never complete as long as we are in this life and we are able to learn from other Christians including, sometimes, very new and simple Christians whose Christian mind is not cluttered up with too many qualifications. It cannot, therefore, be a *complete* system or world-and-life view. We shall all the time be discovering new aspects of it as our life moves on. Even the Bible's systems of ethics and doctrine are not complete, so a Christian mind will be far less complete than either, since it is an application of both to changing situations.

I described the Christian life as a structured or principled ethical system. The overall key concept is love, but love that has a shape in particular commands and principles and a few fixed points. Similarly I described the biblical system of doctrine as a network of truths all revolving round Jesus Christ who is the

Truth. He is the key; but there are particular truths, and they form an open network of principles and not a complete system. The Christian mind is, as a result, what we can develop as we apply these principles to our own thinking, our life, and our society. Christian wisdom starts with "the fear of the Lord," or personal faith in the Lord Jesus Christ. But although that is the beginning of wisdom, it is not the whole of wisdom, and the Christian is, as the old saying has it, "to seek honey even in the lion's mouth." He is to be willing to learn from any source if it fits into the framework of Christian revelation.

Like Joshua, then, we are to face life's issues by meditating on God's Word day and night so that we shall not depart from it to the right hand or to the left. To see how God's truth applies will not always be easy, and we must be glad and willing to store our minds with truths whose practical relevance is not at the moment obvious. The wise man is the one who "brings out of his treasure what is new and what is old" (Matt. 13:52) with real understanding. This means more than collecting a "best thought" out of our Bible reading each day. It means understanding the Bible. Group study is a great help here, especially when it encourages good application. It also means that we are willing to learn from older Christians who have wider experience and biblical knowledge. It means an eagerness to read Christian books that seek honestly to expound and apply the Bible.

7. The Christian mind has no hierarchy of areas of thought, but the New Testament says I am to start with a new attitude to myself and with straightforward personal ethics. To launch into Christian politics, Christian philosophy, or Christian social ethics is not in itself to make any progress in the Christian mind. It can even be a way of escaping from more urgent personal questions about my attitude to my home, my money, my job, or my church. A Christian mind is not primarily academic or philosophical. Wisdom is not only great theological principles; it is also detailed practical application to everyday questions. The *Bible's agenda* must come first.

Nevertheless, the Christian mind is not just a string of rules about particular questions. The New Testament shows that often we have to go a long way behind the detailed questions to ask what basic attitudes, priorities, aspects of truth about God or man or the world, are really at issue. This will not be without mental effort. Even Peter, the least intellectual of the New Testament writers, tells us to gird up the loins of our minds. Insofar as we can we are to try to develop a network of biblical teachings—"a pattern of sound words"—that can help us to steer our way. Here the biblical pattern is at first sight surprisingly open, but astonishingly down to earth and relevant.

8. Finally, why is the Bible not more specific? I suggest that one reason for this is that such a clear-cut application of truth to the issues of the first century A.D. would have been very dangerous. First of all, it would have invited a lapse into a new legalism. Paul often, therefore, refuses to answer yes or no. But second, life is too varied and too changing. Even in the first century the church was operating in more than one culture (Greek and Jewish). As has been said before, a church that is married to the culture of one generation will be a widow in the next. God has deliberately left us the creative freedom to work out how the pattern applies. As no human parent ought to try to define the lifestyle of his grown-up children, but must responsibly give guidelines, so God has given us a framework of thought and priorities that is really extraordinarily general, and yet it is given to us in a shape that makes it possible for people from many educational backgrounds and cultures to live by it with joy. We should have confidence that we have in outline the "good and acceptable and perfect" will of God. The Bible is a sufficient guide even though it does not satisfy the very tidy-minded. Our task is, first, to understand it and store our mind with it and, second, to apply it in a biblical way to the varied and changing situations in which God in his providence places us. The task should be tackled with enthusiasm, knowing that this is one way to please God and to show human beings something of the wonder of his character and his goodness to us.

"Do not be conformed to this world but be transformed by the renewal of your mind, that you may prove what is the will of God, what is good and acceptable and perfect" (Rom. 12:2).

Appendix

The Dooyeweerdian
"Christian philosophy"

Not everyone will be interested in the following pages, but for the sake of completeness and its own intrinsic interest I venture the following comments on this philosophical system. Developed by the "Amsterdam" school in association with the names of Professors Dooyeweerd and Vollenhoven, it provides a good example of a Christian philosophy. It is more than Christian philosophical thinking; it is a complete system. First let it be said that this school asks some excellent questions and must be admired for its attempt to deal with important issues. One must be thankful for the intellectual effort that Christians have put into it and for those very important elements that have a solid biblical base. As a critique from a Christian standpoint of other philosophical systems it is very useful. It has, however, several important weaknesses. After criticizing other systems it has never been able to put an altogether satisfactory system in their place. As I have explained, I believe that this is because a complete Christian philosophical system is not possible. But my particular criticisms are as follows.

First, its advocates speak as if philosophy was prior to theology and should control our understanding of revelation. That of course could happen; but the Bible method of dealing with this is to work from truth revealed in the Bible outward, not to work from a revised philosophy as fresh spectacles through which to view Christian revelation. By all means let those who can do battle in this area work outward from theology into the area of philosophy. To be shown that we have sometimes (usually unconsciously) adopted unbiblical views because they are part of our cultural heritage (which itself has been molded by wrong philosophies) is important. We need to be alerted if we have not seen how the biblical revelation refutes and replaces them with something different. Some of these issues can rightly be called philosophical issues, and some dangerously misleading ideas that arise from the writers of popular philosophy have a wide influence. But the remedy lies first of all in biblical truth—that is to say in theology. The New Testament never urges us to develop a philosophical system as in any way important for living out the Christian life. It always urges us to go back to revealed truth (theology).

Second, the system that has been developed—like many philosophical systems—is artificial in the extreme from a biblical point of view. There are, according to this philosophy, fifteen "law spheres" into which reality can be divided. The result is a sort of complex "complementarity" scheme with areas of thought each having to some extent their own independent concepts, rules, and kinds of truth.

This philosophy may be a very perceptive observation of how the world works and a useful classification of reality, but no one can possibly say that it is found in the Bible or that other classifications with more or fewer than fifteen law spheres might not be better from a biblical standpoint. Neither have we *biblical* grounds for preferring the "law sphere" concept to other alternative ways of doing much the same thing. Karl Heim's "spaces" and the "dimensions" of D. M. MacKay and other writers, for instance, are really grappling with many of the same problems in a similar way. All of these are very interesting intellectual ways of dividing up reality so that we can proceed to deal with it effectively. The Dooyeweerdian system is what it professes to be—a philosophical system. It is based to a considerable extent on Christian thinking; but much of it is what we have called guesswork (or shortcuts), and in some areas it has now been shown not to work well. As we said earlier, anything that fills in the gaps on the map or develops intellectual shortcuts is bound to bring some distortion of reality and is never certain ground.

Third, this system seems to claim too much. Dooyeweerd and his followers often stress the almost total antithesis between Christian and non-Christian thinking. On page 572 of his *New Critique of Theoretical Thought* Dooyeweerd admits that non-Christians are faced with undeniable states of affairs within the world and can discover relative truths. Yet he also insists there are no such "loose" moments of truth since "all relative truths within the temporal horizon are only true in the *fullness* of Verity revealed by God in Christ. Any absolutizing of that which is relative, turns truth into falsehood. Even the judgment; two times two equals four becomes an untruth if . . . detached from the temporal world order and from the sovereignty of God as the Creator."

This almost total antithesis is, however, very difficult to detect in practice in most areas of study. This is especially so in those areas that are furthest away from personal motivation such as mathematics and the more impersonal sciences. To take, for example, his statement about two times two equals four: the fact is that Christian mathematicians have not shown themselves notably closer to the reality of God's creation in the mathematical world than have other mathematicians. If they alone understand it correctly, they should do better mathematics. Not only do they not do visibly better mathematics, but what they do is indistinguishable from the mathematics done by others. The same could be said of many sciences, and in Holland, where he developed his thinking, Professor Dooyeweerd had great difficulty in persuading Christian scientists to adopt it. In areas of thought that have a large philosophical or ethical aspect, of course, the differences between Christian and non-Christian thinking may be obvious; but this is something quite different from having a total antithesis.

It seems that Dooyeweerd confused two things—how the Christian *interprets* reality and how he *knows* reality. In his early writing, as Brümmer has shown, he stressed the former. Only later was he pushed, by attempts to be intellectually consistent, into the apparently false claim that only the Christian *knows* reality accurately. Quite apart from the fact that it does not seem to work out as he suggests, the position he adopts has failed to come to terms with one great biblical truth. He does not seem to have accepted the biblical view of wisdom or what is said in Romans 1 and 2 about the non-Christian having a knowledge of God and a knowledge of morality even if, to a large extent, they are suppressed. His philosophy has (in the interests of consistency) pushed him into a false shortcut here. Put in another way, the Dooyeweerdian system does not give sufficient room to what in the Dutch Reformed tradition is called "common grace." The fact is that, in God's goodness, non-Christians do discover great and useful things. We are thankful to God for those who discovered penicillin, and it does not matter whether they were Christians or not. They discovered some *truths* about reality which are extremely useful. Paul can say to a fellow Christian about a pagan poet's judgment, "This testimony is true" (Titus 1:13). Non-Christians do, according to the Bible, know some truths. They do have some limited but real "wisdom" (see chapter 5, above).

Fourth, because the system is a philosophy, Dooyeweerd makes the starting point the regenerate heart of man. The Christian, however, ought to make God and not man the starting point of his thinking. He wants to make revelation and not the things that man (even regenerate man) can perceive the basis of this understanding. As we have said, this is frankly to develop a theology rather than a philosophy. If having a philosophy involves starting our thinking with man rather than God, then we have to say that this already has some dangerous inbuilt distortions before the system begins to develop. However ingenious it may be, a Christian philosophy like this is just a department of human science.

Finally, the institutions which it has fathered and the practical policies to which it leads are not impressive for their Christian fruitfulness and are often controversial from a biblical point of view. Other people who are innocent of all Christian philosophy have done at least equally well, because they were ruled by revealed truth in a more straightforward way. As we have said, it repeatedly raised expectations which it cannot fulfill and left the straightforward Christian feeling a little inferior. I believe, in fact, that the straightforward Christian should know that he has the key to life's problems, given to him in Scripture, and that he will make greater progress in the application of biblical truth if he follows the agenda and method of the Bible than if he tries to build something so abstruse and difficult to understand as a Christian philosophy. Joshua and Paul are his models here, not Thomas Aquinas.

Having said that, let me repeat that I believe there is a need for Christian thinking in the area of philosophy, and that these philosophers have done some of that thinking in a way that is very helpful to those who are trying to do battle in the field of philosophy. I do not believe that their attempt to erect a Christian philosophy is a success, but that does not mean that they have not some other very useful things to say to philosophers.

DATE DUE
